GREEN BEANS
and
GUACAMOLE

A COLLECTION OF FAVORITE RECIPES *from Houston's Top Restaurants & Their Chefs*

written by **MARIA GLYMPH** and **NATALIE BOGAN MORGAN**

photography by **SHANNON O'HARA**, **DEBORA SMAIL** and **JULIE SOEFER**

book design by Matthew Pacetti, **GOOD PROJECT**

A project by **Friends for Good**, a 501(3)c organization, benefiting **The Arc**

GreenBeansandGuacamole.com

published by Friesens. Manitoba, Canada

Copyright © 2012 by Friends for Good
photography Copyright © 2012 by Shannon O'Hara, Debora Smail and Julie Soefer
(SEE BELOW FOR INDIVIDUAL IMAGE CREDITS)

ISBN 978-0-615-51439-0

Library of Congress Control Number: 2011938266

10 9 8 7 6 5 4 3 2 1

Printed in Canada

SHANNON O'HARA

Photos featured on pages 12-17: Armandos; 18, 19: Ava; 44: Brennan's; 46-51: The Cafe at Brookwood; 53: Canopy; 56-61: Carrabba's; 80-85: Cullen's; 86-91: Damian's; 96-101: Frank's; 108, 109: Haven; 114, 115: Hugo's; 138-142: Le Mistral; 174-179: Ouisie's Table; 186, 187, 189, 191: Philippe; 206: Rainbow Lodge; 208-213: Ray's Country Gourmet; 224-229: Ristorante Cavour; 230, 231: Shade; 240-243: Sorrel; Back Cover: Le Mistral

DEBORA SMAIL

Photos featured on pages 2: Foreword; 30, 31: benjy's; 34-39: Bistro Alex; 40-43: Brennan's; 68-73: Coppa; 74-79: Crapitto's; 92, 93: Feast; 110-113: Haven; 120-125: Ibiza; 126-131: Indika; 132-137: Kiran's; 144-149: Mark's; 150-155: Masraff's; 162, 163: Mockingbird Bistro; 168-173: Olivette; 192-197: Piatto; 198, 199: Quattro; 234-239: Slow Dough; 246-251: Sorrento; 274-279: Zelko; 284: Appendix; 286: Index; 288-289

JULIE SOEFER

Photos featured on pages 3: Foreword; 6-11: Américas; 20, 21: Ava; 22-27: Backstreet Cafe; 28-30, 32, 33: benjy's; 52-55: Canopy; 62-67: Ciao Bello; 94, 95: Feast; 102-107: Gigi's; 108, 109: Haven; 114-119: Hugo's; 156-161: Max's Wine Dive; 164-167: Mockingbird Bistro; 180-185: Pappas Restaurants; 200-203: Quattro; 204, 205: Rainbow Lodge; 214-217: RDG; 218-223: Reef; 232, 233: Shade; 252-257: t'afia; 258-261: The Grove; 262-267: Tony's; 268-273: Tony Mandola's

THANK YOU TO THE **GENEROUS HOUSTON RESTAURANTS** THAT BELIEVED IN OUR VISION AND SUPPORTED THIS PROJECT, as well as to the remarkable group of volunteers who tested every recipe and worked tirelessly to raise the funds needed to produce *Green Beans and Guacamole*. Without their dedication and support, our vision would not have become a reality. For a list of volunteers, please see the Acknowledgements on pages 282-283.

TABLE OF CONTENTS

FOREWORD

by **JEFF GREMILLION,** editor-in-chief of *Houston* magazine

This is a book about the best restaurants in Houston, with glimpses into the coolest kitchens around. It's filled with timely and terrific recipes from H-Town's best chefs and with gorgeous pictures taken by the region's top food photographers. It's a dream-come-true tome for anybody who wants to be up to date on how we dine out, cook and entertain in the fourth-largest city in the United States of America.

So it's a little weird that, when I think about my new friend Austin Hanson, the bespectacled and sandy-blond-headed people person who inspired this ambitious project, I don't think first about food, but rather dancing.

"Oh, you're getting that?" laughs his mom, Belinda Hillhouse, a sales consultant at Houston's M Penner clothing boutique, as we three meet over sodas at a Galleria café to discuss *Green Beans and Guacamole.* That, of course, is this book, which she and her advertising-agency pal Mina Mann conceived of a couple years ago, as a way to raise funds to support two area nonprofits that look after the interests and promote the wellbeing of kids and adults who, like 25-year-old Austin, have some form of intellectual or developmental disability.

It's not that Austin isn't into cooking. He is. Loves chefs, loves their kitchens. All he asked for his 13th birthday was to tour a restaurant kitchen. "Mesmerized," says Belinda. Ever since, he's enjoyed dining out and meeting restaurateurs and cooks, and also helping cook at home. His repertoire ranges from an accomplished balsamic vinaigrette to hearty, old-school meatloaf.

He even likes to plan dinner events and entertain. Green beans and guacamole, in fact, made up the menu for the surprise party he organized (with the help of his grandparents) to celebrate his mom's birthday a few years back. He used his tip money— he's been bagging groceries for six years at Brookshire Brothers grocery store, not far from the Katy home he shares with his mom and his step-dad Corky Hillhouse—to buy the flowers and a cake that read, quite thoroughly, "Happy Birthday Belinda Hillhouse."

But Austin—a hand-shaking, shoulder-clasping junior Good Ol' Boy with a downright presidential knack for coining his own superlatives like "outstandable," and who begins anecdotes by leaning in close, smiling widely and announcing, "Let me tell you the story..."— never beams so brightly as when he talks about the dances he regularly attends at The Arc of Katy, one of the book's beneficiaries. "I like parties," he says matter-of-factly. "We dance our knees off."

The young man and his folks have relied on Arc since Austin was nine weeks old. "I was 26 when Austin was born," recalls Belinda, an elegantly put-together blonde, who balances mom and work duties with genial aplomb, and who clearly dotes on her boy. "My insurance wouldn't have covered everything he needed. I wouldn't have known what to do or how to do it."

Luckily, Arc knew. And, at very little cost to Belinda, the organization started the infant in speech, physical and occupational therapies long before he could even crawl. It also provided opportunities for summer camps and the like as he got older. The result has been what's known as a "mainstreamed" life for a great kid.

Besides graduating from Katy High School and getting his job, Austin plays golf and bowls ("I've beat my dad a couple times"), enjoys an active social life, and does all kinds of civic-minded volunteer work around Katy, where he's known as the "half-mayor." He says, "I like to work. I like to take care of people who are sick. I take care of family and friends."

And every now and then he takes care of himself, too, indulging in the summer of 2011, in a cruise to the Bahamas with other young adults from the Arc of Greater Houston, the other group that the sales of this book helps. The Houston Arc's mission is similar to the one in Katy. Both offer a range of services and programs to suit the unique needs of folks like Austin and also those whose disabilities are more severe, requiring more intensive and constant support.

With that in mind, one can be sure that the proceeds from this book will go far to improve the lives and raise the spirits of special-needs children, adults and their families. But, believe me, buying a copy ought not be a dutiful, eat-your-spinach kinda thing. More like, eat your shrimp corndog with "Tabasco mash" rémoulade, which is one of the recipes chef Randy Evans of Haven restaurant offers. Nearly 50 other chefs also pitched in, like Soren Pedersen of Hillhouse fave Ray's Country Gourmet in Fulshear and also of Sorrel Urban Bistro, which recently opened near River Oaks.

"It's great to meet someone like Austin, who has such a good spirit and who really has such an excitement about food," says Soren, who moved to Houston years ago from Denmark by way of Seattle. "When he comes in, he always wants to try new things and learn. He's so much fun to be around—so honest and sincere. It rubs off on other people, or at least it does on me." Herein, the chef offers recipes for grilled rack of lamb sauced with a red currant demi-glace, and for a tart with pears and marzipan.

Unlike many charity cookbooks, however, this book doesn't just have home-tested recipes for great dishes. It also has stunning, magazine-worthy photos of them. And, as the editor-in-chief of *Houston* magazine, I am qualified to say so. In fact, my own involvement in this project stems primarily from my association with the people who took the pictures; Julie Soefer, Shannon O'Hara and Debora Smail contribute many of the best photographs in the magazine month after month, and their food photos are, hands down, the best you'll see anywhere in these parts.

"I love it," says Shannon, of regularly working in H-Town restaurants. "There is so much diversity here and it's all done on a level that easily rivals that of any other large city in the world. I'm excited to be here shooting as Houston gains more international attention for its amazing culinary scene."

O'Hara also found teaming up with his magazine colleagues to help Austin and both Arc chapters to be a great reward. Which is good, because he did not avail himself of the reward I myself would have, had I been in his shoes—the grub itself! "I get offered to eat what I shoot all the time, but I rarely take advantage of that. I don't like looking like the tacky food photographer who sucks down every

dish that passes in front of his camera! But take a look at some of the dishes in this book and you'll understand how I could have let myself go."

Julie puts it more succinctly: "If I ate everything I shot, I would be a cow, not a photographer.

"It's great to be collaborating with my two fellow *Houston* mag photographers," adds Julie, who was actually the first of the photographers to get involved in the cookbook enterprise. "I think this could pave the way for future projects for us together. Next year could be *Kumquats and Potatoes*."

Could be. But today it's all about green beans, guacamole and a cool dude named Austin. So fire up the stove and strike up the band. Let's dance and let's eat. Aw heck, let's party. I mean, we might as well, because you know he sure will.

In fact, today in this bright café, as we wrap up our meeting, he leans over, pushes his glasses just a little ways up his nose, gives me a knowing wink, and tells me convincingly that the entire notion is absolutely, positively *outstandable*.

GREEN BEANS

and

GUACAMOLE

A COLLECTION OF FAVORITE RECIPES *from Houston's Top Restaurants & Their Chefs*

AMÉRICAS

Chef and restaurateur Michael Cordua merges the bold, rich flavors of South America with touches of the Caribbean and Mexico at his award-winning Américas restaurant. The venture, which has a location in River Oaks Shopping Center and another in The Woodlands, shares an innovative menu that is dramatic and bold. Entrées like plantain-crusted shrimp and quail taquitos draw fast fans, though it's Américas churrasco—named *Esquire* magazine's "Top 20 Steaks in America"—and the original tres leches that remains Chef Cordua's food frontrunners. Outfitted in eye-popping, new-age architecture, both locations are lively and exotic, drawing an eclectic clientele that craves artisan cocktails, South American vino and top-notch cuisine.

GREEN BEANS AND GUACAMOLE

MARINATED TOMATOES & CHEESE

1	CUP EXTRA VIRGIN OLIVE OIL
1	TEASPOON KOSHER SALT
1	TEASPOON FRESH GARLIC, CHOPPED
½	TEASPOON RED PEPPER FLAKE
4	MEDIUM VINE-RIPENED TOMATOES, SLICED IN 16, ½-INCH SLICES
1	POUND FRESH MOZZARELLA, SLICED IN 16, ½-INCH SLICES

JALAPEÑO MAYONNAISE

16	OUNCES MAYONNAISE
2½	OUNCES RED PEPPER, DICED ¼-INCH
1	OUNCE GREEN ONION, DICED ¼-INCH
2½	OUNCES YELLOW ONION, DICED ¼-INCH
1	PINCH RED PEPPER FLAKE
1	PINCH KOSHER SALT
1	OUNCE LIME JUICE

CRAB SALAD

16	OUNCES JUMBO LUMP CRAB
½	CUP JALAPEÑO MAYONNAISE
1	TABLESPOON FRESH TARRAGON, CHOPPED
3	TABLESPOONS BASIL CHIFFONADE

CRAB CAPRICHOSA

2	AVOCADOS, PEELED AND SLICED INTO 12 SLICES
16	MARINATED TOMATO SLICES
16	MARINATED FRESH MOZZARELLA SLICES
16	OUNCES CRAB SALAD
1	TABLESPOON BASIL CHIFFONADE

serves 4

TO PREPARE THE TOMATOES & CHEESE
Combine first four ingredients in a mixing bowl. Place sliced tomatoes and sliced fresh mozzarella into separate bowls. Pour half of the marinade into each bowl to cover the tomatoes and cheese. Wrap and refrigerate for at least one hour or up to 6 hours.

TO PREPARE THE JALAPEÑO MAYONNAISE
Combine all ingredients in a mixing bowl. Mix well to incorporate. Can be made in advance and will keep for 5 days.

TO PREPARE THE CRAB SALAD
Combine jalapeño mayonnaise, tarragon and basil in a mixing bowl. Gently fold in crabmeat to incorporate and coat evenly with mayonnaise.

TO PREPARE THE CRAB CAPRICHOSA
Arrange 1 slice of tomato, 1 slice of cheese, 1 slice of avocado on a plate. Repeat 3 more times for each plate. Arrange 4 ounces of crab salad over the layered tomato, cheese and avocado. Garnish with basil chiffonade. Drizzle 1 teaspoon of marinade from tomatoes over each plate as additional garnish.

GREEN BEANS AND GUACAMOLE

COCOA TART
AMERICAS

COCOA TART SHELLS

4	OUNCES BUTTER, WHOLE, UNSALTED
3½	OUNCES GRANULATED SUGAR
10	OUNCES ALL-PURPOSE FLOUR
2	OUNCES HERSHEY'S COCOA POWDER
1	EGG YOLK

SEMI-SWEET GANACHE

16	OUNCES SEMI-SWEET CHOCOLATE CHIPS
16	OUNCES HEAVY WHIPPING CREAM

DARK GANACHE

16	OUNCES CHOCOLATE, GIANDUJA CACAO BAR, SEE NOTE
16	OUNCES HEAVY WHIPPING CREAM

TOPPING

4	OUNCES PEANUTS, CHOPPED FINE
16	OUNCES COCONUT ICE CREAM
8	OUNCES CRACKER JACKS

serves 8

Preheat oven to 325°F.

TO PREPARE THE COCOA TART SHELLS
Dice butter into small cubes, allow to adjust to room temperature. In a mixer with a paddle attachment, cream butter, sugar and egg yolk at medium speed for 20 minutes. Meanwhile, sift dry ingredients together in a separate bowl. Reduce speed on mixing bowl to low. Add dry ingredients, mix at low speed for 1 minute, then increase to medium for 3 minutes. Remove dough from mixer, wrap and chill for 1 hour. Then remove dough from cooler and allow to adjust to room temperature. Portion dough into 2-ounce balls. Using a tortilla press, lined with plastic wrap, press each portioned dough into flat, round discs. Each disc should look like a chocolate tortilla. Spray 3-inch, non-stick tart mold with pan coating spray. Press flattened dough into mold. Ensure all cracks are sealed with dough. Trim edges so that dough does not come over the edge of the mold. Using a fork, poke bottom of each shell a couple of times to avoid bubbling during baking. Bake at 325°F for 5 minutes. Remove from oven and allow to cool to room temperature before filling.

TO PREPARE THE SEMI SWEET OR DARK GANACHE
Instructions are applicable to either version. Place cream in a saucepan and bring to low boil. Place chocolate chips in a mixing bowl. Add hot cream to chips and stir well to melt chocolate completely. Allow to cool. Ganache can be reheated for filling the tart shells in a microwave. Depending on the microwave, 30 seconds should be long enough to return ganache to liquid consistency.

TO PREPARE THE COCOA TARTS
Warm dark ganache until pourable, pour 1.25 ounces into bottom of each tart shell. Place in freezer for 30 minutes to set. Next, warm the semi-sweet ganache until pourable, pour 1.25 ounce into tart shell, filling to top. Place in cooler over night to set ganache. Once cooled overnight, turn shell over in hand to release from mold, it should pop right out. If not, place mold upside down on heat-proof surface and warm with brûlée torch gently until tart releases from the mold. Place each completed tart onto its plate. Pass the lit brûlée torch over the top, which gives the ganache a nice sheen. Place chopped peanuts next to each tart and top with coconut ice cream. Garnish tart with Cracker Jacks before serving.

NOTE: Gianduja cacao bar can be purchased online or found locally.

ARMANDOS

Armando Palacios' Upper Kirby
namesake is as famous for its
upscale Mexican fare as it is for
its see-and-be-seen clientele.
The iconic restaurant has been
a style staple among well-heeled
Houstonians and celebrities for
decades. Inside, the softly-lit
interior is elegant and inviting,
marked by shimmering antique
mirrors, ocher-hued walls and
dark-wood accents. White linen-
topped tables set the stage for
Armandos' famously-potent
margaritas, verde-sauce-topped
enchiladas and the eatery's
signature appetizer—mushroom-
flecked queso flameado paired
with piping-hot tortillas. For a
sizzling party on wheels, look for
Armandos' famed taco truck,
often parked just outside the
Upper Kirby outpost. The one-of-
a-kind catering truck is outfitted
with Wolf Appliances, chrome
accents and the restaurant's
signature shade of red.

CEVICHE
ARMANDOS

4	SKINLESS TILAPIA FILLETS, CUBED
1¼	POUNDS COOKED SHRIMP, SLICED IN HALF
½	CUP LIME JUICE
2	CUPS WATER
½	BUNCH CILANTRO, CHOPPED
4	ROMA TOMATOES, DICED
1½	TABLESPOONS TABASCO SAUCE
½	MEDIUM YELLOW ONION, DICED SMALL
1-2	JALAPEÑOS, DICED
5	GREEN OLIVES, CHOPPED
	SALT
1	LARGE RIPE AVOCADO, PEELED, PITTED AND THINLY SLICED FOR GARNISH
	TORTILLA CHIPS OR SALTINE CRACKERS, FOR SERVING

serves 10

In a large plastic bowl, combine the tilapia, shrimp, lime juice and a pinch of salt. Pour enough of the water over the mixture to cover all of the fish. Additional water may be needed. Cover the bowl and refrigerate for a minimum of five hours. Drain the tilapia and shrimp in a colander and place in a bowl. Add the remaining ingredients, except the avocado, and toss gently. Season with salt and additional lime juice, if needed. Garnish with avocado. Serve cold, along with tortilla chips or saltine crackers.

NOTE: Either Manzanilla or Queen olives will impart authentic Mexican flavor.

FLAN
ARMANDOS

CARAMEL

1½	CUPS SUGAR
¼	CUP WATER

FLAN

12	EGGS
3	CUPS MILK
2	CUPS HEAVY CREAM
1	VANILLA BEAN
1	CUP SUGAR

serves 12

Preheat oven to 350°F.

TO PREPARE THE CARAMEL
Melt the sugar over medium heat, stirring occasionally, until the sugar has dissolved and turns a medium, dark amber color. Remove from heat and stir in the water. Immediately divide caramel into 12 ramekins and swirl to coat bottom and partially up sides.

TO PREPARE THE FLAN
Bring the milk, heavy cream and the vanilla bean to a simmer over medium heat. Do not boil. In a separate bowl, gently whisk the eggs and sugar. Slowly add the warmed milk mixture, stirring gently until all of the liquid is well integrated. Ladle the custard into the ramekins. Place the ramekins in a hot water bath that reaches half way up the sides. Bake for approximately 1 hour 20 minutes or until the flan sets. Remove the ramekins from the water and refrigerate for 5 hours. Unmold just before serving.

NOTE: To extract more flavor, split the vanilla bean lengthwise and scrape the seeds into the saucepan, before adding the pod.

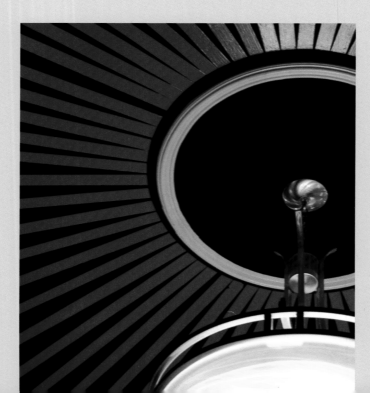

AVA
KITCHEN & WHISKEY BAR

In Robert del Grande's latest culinary venture, the storied chef offers up American and Mediterranean favorites inside a contemporary, West Ave-set space. Fuchsia banquettes and cornflower-blue accents add to the eye-catching interior, as do dramatic windows and veneer pendant lights that hang overhead. Ava's menu shines, too, touting grilled-stuffed squid with shrimp sausage and linguine Granchio with Gulf crab and fisherman's broth. For a more casual, come-as-you-are off-spin, head upstairs to Alto Pizzeria—the second half of Robert del Grande's West Ave creation. There, guests find stone-oven-fired designer pizzas that range from the classic Margherita to the Gorgonzola pie, topped with white cheese, bacon-dried mission figs and arugula.

GREEN BEANS AND GUACAMOLE

GRAPEFRUIT AND BUTTERMILK SOUP
with shrimp, avocado and jicama

SOUP

2	PINK GRAPEFRUITS, JUICED, APPROXIMATELY 1½ CUPS
2	TEASPOONS PINK GRAPEFRUIT ZEST
	PINCH SUGAR
1	CUP BUTTERMILK
4	TABLESPOONS HEAVY CREAM OR SUBSTITUTE YOGURT
2	TABLESPOONS CILANTRO, CHOPPED
1	TEASPOON SALT
¼	TEASPOON BLACK PEPPER

GARNISHES

8	OUNCES COOKED SHRIMP, CUT INTO CUBES
1	CUP JICAMA, PEELED AND CUT INTO SMALL CUBES
1	AVOCADO, PEELED, SEEDED AND CUT INTO SMALL CUBES
½	SERRANO PEPPER, VERY THINLY SLICED
1	TABLESPOON EXTRA VIRGIN OLIVE OIL

serves 4

TO PREPARE THE SOUP
Combine all ingredients in a medium bowl and stir to mix well. Adjust seasonings if necessary. Chill for several hours.

TO SERVE
Distribute the garnishes among 4 soup bowls. Ladle the soup over the garnishes. With a small spoon, drop small droplets of the extra virgin olive oil over the surface of the soup and serve.

NOTE: For zesting and juicing the grapefruit, use a potato peeler. Remove the zests from the grapefruits and finely mince to yield approximately 4 teaspoons. Cut the grapefruits in half and juice. Remove any seeds, but capture a little of the pulp.

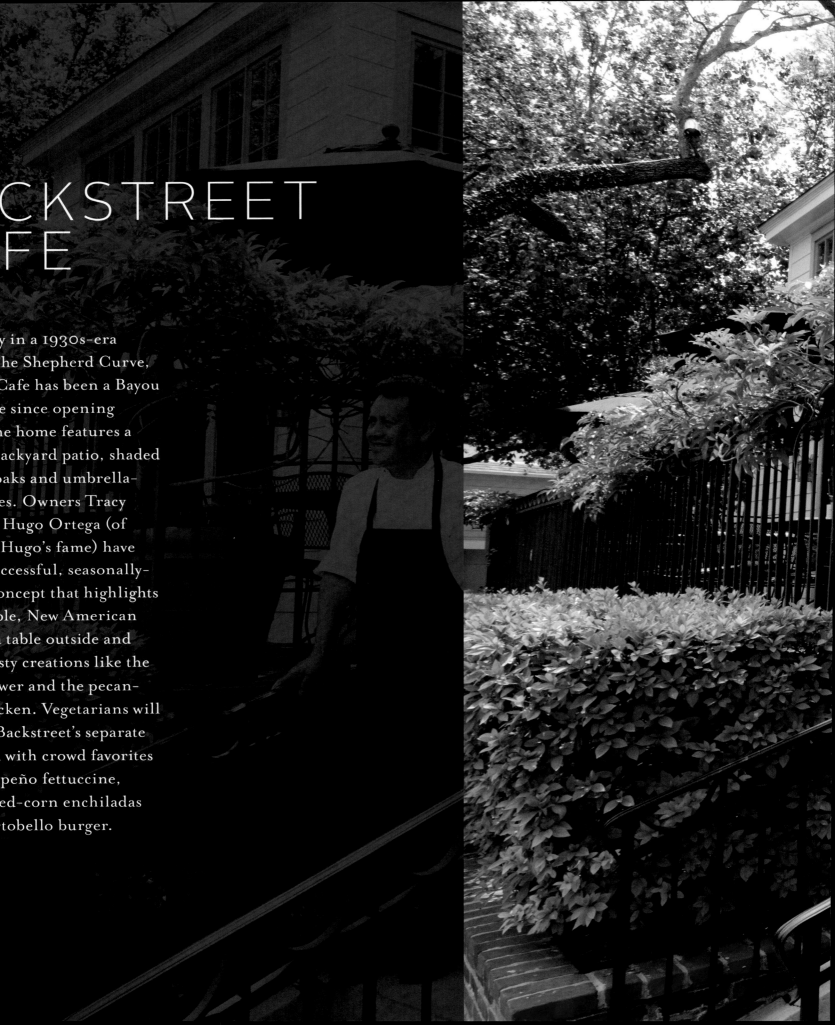

CKSTREET
FE

y in a 1930s-era
he Shepherd Curve,
Cafe has been a Bayou
e since opening
he home features a
ackyard patio, shaded
aks and umbrella-
es. Owners Tracy
Hugo Ortega (of
Hugo's fame) have
ccessful, seasonally-
oncept that highlights
le, New American
table outside and
sty creations like the
wer and the pecan-
cken. Vegetarians will
Backstreet's separate
with crowd favorites
peño fettuccine,
ed-corn enchiladas
tobello burger.

ARTICHOKE SOUP
BACKSTREET CAFE

1	OUNCE BUTTER
¼	CUP GARLIC, CHOPPED
¼	CUP SHALLOTS, CHOPPED
2	SPRIGS BASIL, CHOPPED
¼	BUNCH PARSLEY, CHOPPED
1	POUND ARTICHOKE HEARTS, UNCOOKED, MEDIUM DICE
2	CUPS CHAMPAGNE
1	POBLANO PEPPER, ROASTED, PEELED AND SEEDED
4	CUPS WHOLE MILK
1	CUP MASHED POTATOES, SEE NOTE
¼	BUNCH WATERCRESS, LEAVES ONLY
	SALT AND PEPPER

serves 4–6

Melt the butter in a pot over medium heat. Add the garlic and shallots, allowing them to sweat for about 3 to 5 minutes or until soft. Add the basil, parsley and artichoke hearts. Cook for 10 to 15 minutes or until the artichokes are soft. Add the Champagne and let it reduce for 10 minutes. Add the poblano pepper. Remove from stove and cool over an ice bath. Add milk and watercress before transferring the soup to a blender. Add the mashed potatoes. Process all ingredients until they are well incorporated and the soup has reached a smooth consistency. Season with salt and pepper.

NOTE: See appendix for a basic mashed potato recipe. Frozen artichoke hearts can be used as an alternative to fresh and make the recipe easier. To ensure a beautiful green color, cool the soup before adding the watercress. Serve with a dollop of cream and top with crispy fried artichoke bottom shavings.

GREEN BEANS AND GUACAMOLE

1	POUND HEIRLOOM TOMATOES, CHOPPED INTO CHUNKS
½	POUND CHERRY TOMATOES, HALVED
½	POUND YELLOW TEAR DROP TOMATOES, HALVED
¼	BUNCH FRESH CILANTRO, CHOPPED
¼	WHITE ONION, SLICED PAPER THIN
1	CUCUMBER, ABOUT 10 OUNCES, PEELED AND DICED
½	POUND YELLOW CORN, ROASTED, KERNELS REMOVED
¾	CUP RADISHES, JULIENNED
1	AVOCADO, PEELED, SEEDED AND DICED
2	TABLESPOONS FRESH LIME JUICE
2	TABLESPOONS VALENTINA SAUCE, SEE NOTE
2	TABLESPOONS OLIVE OIL
	SALT
	TORTILLA CHIPS, FOR SERVING

serves 6–8

Gently mix all ingredients in a bowl. Season with salt and serve with chips—a very refreshing, light and flavorful cocktail.

NOTE: Valentina sauce is a brand of hot sauce that can be found at local grocery stores.

GREEN BEANS AND GUACAMOLE

BENJY'S

GREEN BEANS AND GUACAMOLE

Hip, young things have flocked to benjy's since the modern American concept first opened in Rice Village in 1995. The lively restaurant has since added a second, larger location on bustling Washington Avenue. Both elegantly-appointed spots draw faithful crowds for nightly happy hours and menus filled with Asian and Latin-inspired cuisine. benjy's culinary line-up changes regularly and reflects dishes that are unique to each location—the seared scallops and seared ahi tuna shine at the Washington locale, while the wood-roasted half chicken and smoked salmon sashimi stand out in West U. Find the professional set in the upstairs lounge or on the patio, sipping signature cocktails like the citrus blossom martini or the blood orange margarita.

BENJYS

CHOCOLATE CAKE

1	CUP WATER
½	POUND MARGARINE
3	OUNCES HERSHEY'S COCOA, BY VOLUME
2	EGGS
2	CUPS SUGAR
1	TEASPOON BAKING SODA
½	TEASPOON SALT
1	TEASPOON VANILLA EXTRACT
2	CUPS ALL-PURPOSE FLOUR
½	CUP BUTTERMILK

CHOCOLATE FROSTING

3	OUNCES MILK, BY VOLUME
¼	POUND MARGARINE
3	OUNCES HERSHEY'S COCOA, BY VOLUME
1	POUND POWDERED SUGAR
1	TEASPOON VANILLA EXTRACT
	PECAN PIECES, FOR TOPPING

serves 8–10

Preheat oven to 350°F.
Grease a 9" x 13" cake pan and set aside.

TO PREPARE THE CAKE
Bring the water, margarine and Hershey's cocoa to a boil. Reduce heat and simmer for 5 minutes, set aside and cool to room temperature. In a large bowl, beat the eggs, sugar, baking soda, salt and vanilla extract for 5 minutes. Alternate adding the flour and buttermilk. Fold in the cocoa and margarine mixture. Pour into prepared cake pan and bake for 20 to 25 minutes or until tester inserted into the center of the cake comes out clean.

TO PREPARE THE FROSTING
In a medium bowl, combine the powdered sugar and vanilla extract. Set aside. Melt the milk, margarine and Hershey's cocoa and add it to the sugar mixture. Stir until smooth and well incorporated. Pour the frosting over the warm cake and spread evenly. Sprinkle pecan pieces over the cake and press them into the frosting.

GREEN BEANS AND GUACAMOLE

2	TABLESPOONS OLIVE OIL
	KERNELS FROM 1 EAR OF CORN
1	TEASPOON GARLIC, MINCED
¾	POUND GOAT CHEESE, ROOM TEMPERATURE
1	OUNCE CREAM CHEESE
¼	CUP SUNDRIED TOMATOES, FINELY CHOPPED
1	TABLESPOON PARSLEY, CHOPPED
	SALT AND PEPPER
2	CUPS SHELLED PISTACHIOS
2	CUPS PANKO (JAPANESE BREAD CRUMBS)
	CRACKERS OR BREAD, FOR SERVING, SEE NOTE
	FRUIT-BASED SAUCE OR JAM, FOR SERVING, SEE NOTE

serves 8–10

Sauté garlic and corn in oil until corn is cooked, but not brown (about 5 minutes). Set aside to cool. In a large bowl, combine the goat cheese, cream cheese, sundried tomatoes and parsley. When corn is cool, add it to the cheese mixture and season with salt and pepper. In a food processor, pulverize the panko and pistachios until fairly smooth and put into a wide, shallow bowl. Scoop a portion of the cheese mixture, toss in the pistachio mixture and mold into desired shape. Repeat with remainder of mixture. Serve with crackers and jam.

NOTE: These have been a staple on the benjy's menu for more than a decade. They are served with different types of breads and sauces. Serve with a cracker or toast that has a little crunch and accompany with a fruit-based salsa or jam.

GREEN BEANS AND GUACAMOLE

BISTRO ALEX

West Houston's pedestrian-friendly CityCentre development has provided a hip escape for Memorial denizens since opening in 2009, thanks in part to lauded restaurants like Alex Brennan-Martin's Bistro Alex. Set inside the luxurious Hotel Sorella, the dramatic interior is light-filled, blending modern accents with a mix of natural elements. Inside, roughhewn and lacquered mesquite planks line the ceiling, deep banquette seating spans the interior and an open kitchen adds to the energetic atmosphere. On Executive Chef Rolando Soza's bold menu, patrons find vibrant options like the prime ribeye with coffee ganache. Stop by Bistro Alex's street-level Bistro Bar—which features an expansive patio space and eye-catching interior—for pre or post-dinner cocktails.

SCALLOPS & CRAWFISH
with roasted fingerling potatoes and crushed corn sauce

BISTRO ALEX

SCALLOPS & CRAWFISH

4   JUMBO SCALLOPS

1   TEASPOON BUTTER

1   TEASPOON OLIVE OIL

1   CUP ROASTED FINGERLING POTATOES, SEE NOTE

½   CUP BACON VINAIGRETTE

1   CUP COOKED FRESH CRAWFISH TAILS, SEE NOTE

½   CUP CRUSHED CORN SAUCE, WARM

½   CUP BABY ARUGULA

½   LEMON, FOR DRIZZLING

    SALT AND PEPPER

2   WHOLE BOILED FRESH CRAWFISH, FOR GARNISH

BACON VINAIGRETTE

¼   POUND BACON, COOKED

¼   CUP CRYSTAL HOT SAUCE, SEE NOTE

⅛   CUP CANE VINEGAR

½   CUP HONEY

1   CUP OLIVE OIL

    SALT AND PEPPER

CRUSHED CORN SAUCE

3   EARS OF CORN, KERNELS CUT FROM THE COB, COBS RESERVED

¼   ONION

½   CUP SUGAR

2   CLOVES GARLIC

½   LEEK, CHOPPED

½   GALLON WATER

1½   CUPS HEAVY CREAM

½   TABLESPOON TURMERIC

serves 2

TO PREPARE THE BACON VINAIGRETTE
Combine all ingredients except the olive oil in a blender. Purée for 1 minute, then slowly add oil to emulsify. Season with salt and pepper.

TO PREPARE THE CORN SAUCE
Combine corn kernels, cobs, onion, sugar, garlic, leek and water in a large pot. Bring to a boil and then simmer for 1 hour. Stir in the cream and reduce until slightly thick. Remove the corn cobs and discard. Place the broth in a blender and add the turmeric. Purée until smooth, then strain through a fine mesh sieve. Season with salt and pepper. Keep warm.

TO PREPARE THE SCALLOPS & CRAWFISH
Sauté the potatoes and bacon vinaigrette in a pan. Simmer for 30 seconds. Add the crawfish and season with salt and pepper. Set aside. In a separate pan, over high heat, melt the butter and olive oil. Sear the scallops on both sides until brown.

TO SERVE
Ladle corn sauce onto plates. Toss the potato salad with the arugula and spread over the sauce. Drizzle the scallops with lemon juice and place atop the potato salad. Garnish with whole crawfish.

NOTE: Fingerling potatoes can be cut lengthwise, tossed in olive oil and roasted at 350°F for approximately 15 to 20 minutes. If crawfish are out of season, substitute with shrimp. Crystal hot sauce is a Louisiana sauce and can be found in most grocery stores. Cane vinegar may be difficult to find and can be substituted with rice vinegar.

GREEN BEANS AND GUACAMOLE

TO PREPARE THE GANACHE
Combine all ingredients in a large pot. Bring to a boil and then simmer until reduced to thick syrup.

TO PREPARE THE WAFFLE
Grill the green onions until tender. Set aside. Sauté the duck, cranberry jam and Swiss chard until heated through. Set aside. In a non-stick pan, fry the quail egg—sunny side up—and season with salt and pepper. Remove from heat.

TO PREPARE THE FOIE FONDUE
Reduce cream by half, transfer to a blender. Add in cubed, cold foie gras. Season with salt and pepper and add Sherry.

TO SERVE
Drizzle the foie fondue on the plate. Place the waffle over the foie fondue and top with duck mix. Position quail egg on waffle and garnish with the green onion. Drizzle all with the chicory coffee ganache.

NOTE: To prepare waffles, add ¼ cup butternut squash to basic waffle recipe or mix.

BUTTERNUT SQUASH & DUCK WAFFLE

2	BUTTERNUT SQUASH WAFFLES, SEE NOTE
1	CUP DUCK CONFIT
½	CUP CRANBERRY JAM
1	CUP RED SWISS CHARD, CHOPPED
2	GREEN ONIONS
2	QUAIL EGGS
½	CUP FOIE FONDUE, SEE RECIPE
½	CUP CHICORY COFFEE GANACHE
	SALT AND PEPPER

CHICORY COFFEE GANACHE

4	CUPS PREPARED CHICORY COFFEE
2	CUPS LIGHT KARO SYRUP
¼	CUP DARK MOLASSES

FOIE FONDUE

4	CUPS HEAVY CREAM
½	POUND GRADE B FOIE GRAS
2	OUNCES SHERRY
	SALT AND PEPPER

serves 2

BRENNAN'S

Alex Brennan-Martin—of New Orleans' famed Brennan's restaurant family—introduced his Texas Creole cuisine to Houston diners in 1967. The venture quickly earned the restaurateur national accolades and local love—an affection that was amplified after Brennan's John Staub-designed building caught fire during 2008's Hurricane Ike. With 90 percent of the original façade left in tact, the iconic restaurant reopened, following a 17-month renovation. In the fresh space, arched windows were opened, the brick was restored and an upper-level Courtyard Bar was added. Longtime menu favorites live on like the turtle soup and bananas foster, along with new favorites like the bourbon molasses-lacquered bobwhite quail with foie gras apple stuffing.

GREEN BEANS AND GUACAMOLE

GULF OYSTER BLT

GULF OYSTER BLT

	GRAPESEED OIL, AS NEEDED
12	GULF COAST OYSTERS
½	POUND CORN MASA BREADING, SEE RECIPE
12	FRENCH BAGUETTE SLICES, ¼-INCH THICK, TOASTED
2	TABLESPOONS CREOLE SEASONING
½	CUP THREE MUSTARD GLAZE, SEE RECIPE
5	OUNCES BACON MOUSSE, SEE RECIPE
5	CHERRY TOMATOES, SLICED AND LIGHTLY SMOKED
1	SHALLOT, SHAVED THIN
12	BABY ARUGULA LEAVES
1	TABLESPOON SUGAR CANE VINEGAR

CORN MASA BREADING

1	WEIGHT OUNCE MASA HARINA (MASECA)
1½	WEIGHT OUNCES CORN MEAL
2	WEIGHT OUNCES ALL-PURPOSE FLOUR
1	WEIGHT OUNCE CORN STARCH
2½	WEIGHT OUNCES CORN FLOUR

THREE MUSTARD GLAZE

1	CUP CORN SYRUP
½	CUP CREOLE MUSTARD
2	TABLESPOONS PREPARED HORSERADISH
2	TEASPOONS DIJON MUSTARD
1	TEASPOON DRY MUSTARD

BACON MOUSSE

1	CUP ONION, JULIENNED AND CARAMELIZED
1	ROMA TOMATO, HALVED, SMOKED AND SKIN REMOVED
2	TABLESPOONS BACON FAT
½	CUP RENDERED BACON PIECES
½	POUND PHILADELPHIA CREAM CHEESE
	SALT AND PEPPER

serves 4 (appetizer portions)

TO PREPARE BREADING
In a mixing bowl, mix all ingredients and set aside.

TO PREPARE MUSTARD GLAZE
Add all ingredients to a heavy-bottom pot over medium heat. Reduce the mixture by ½ or until it reaches a syrup consistency. Let the glaze cool and transfer to a squeeze bottle.

TO PREPARE MOUSSE
In a food processor, purée the caramelized onions, bacon pieces, bacon fat and smoked tomato until fully ground. Add Philadelphia cream cheese and purée until smooth. Add salt and pepper to taste. Chill in the refrigerator to stiffen the mousse.

TO PREPARE THE GULF OYSTER BLT
Heat the grapeseed oil in a heavy saucepan or deep fryer. The oil should be about 3 inches deep. Dredge the oysters in the corn masa mixture. When the oil reaches 350°F, fry the oysters until they reach a golden brown, about 3 minutes. Season well with Creole seasoning and set aside.

TO SERVE
Spread the bacon mousse, about ½ of a tablespoon, on the toasted baguette slices. Place one oyster on top. On individual plates or a serving platter, squeeze the three mustard glaze in a zigzag motion, then place the oyster crostini on top. In small bowl, mix the baby arugula, shaved shallots, cherry tomatoes, sugar cane vinegar, and season with salt and pepper. Garnish each crostini with one leaf of baby arugula, shallot and cherry tomato. Squeeze a few drops of the three mustard glaze on each oyster.

NOTE: Sugar cane vinegar is available in specialty markets or online. If unavailable, substitute rice vinegar.

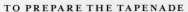

TO PREPARE THE TAPENADE
Combine all ingredients in a bowl and set aside. Yields
2 cups.

TO PREPARE SALAD
Heat olive oil in a sauté pan. Season the tuna with salt and
pepper. Sear tuna on all sides for 1 minute. Transfer to a
plate and refrigerate. In a large bowl, combine the hearts of
palm, beans, peppers and frisée. Season to taste and toss
with half of the olive tapenade. Slice the tuna into 16 slices.

TO SERVE
Place a tomato slice in the center of the plate, top with egg
slices. Then place the salad mix on top of the tomato. Fan 4
slices of tuna across the salad. Drizzle the remaining olive
tapenade around the plate.

NOTE: Tuna can be rolled in mustard seed to form a crust
before searing.

SALAD

2	TABLESPOONS OLIVE OIL
1	POUND SASHIMI-GRADE TUNA, YELLOW OR BLUE FIN
	SALT AND PEPPER
2	TOMATO SLICES, ¼-INCH THICK
¼	CUP HEARTS OF PALM, SLICED LENGTHWISE
1	ROASTED RED BELL PEPPER, JULIENNED
16	FRENCH BEANS OR GREEN BEANS, BLANCHED
1	HEAD FRISÉE LETTUCE
2	EGGS, HARD BOILED, SLICED INTO THICK ROUNDS
¼	CUP OLIVE TAPENADE, SEE RECIPE

OLIVE TAPENADE

1½	CUPS BLACK OLIVES, MINCED
¼	CUP SHALLOTS, MINCED
1	TABLESPOON GARLIC, MINCED
¼	CUP ANCHOVY, MINCED
2	TABLESPOONS PARSLEY, CHOPPED
2	TABLESPOONS CAPERS, CHOPPED
½	LEMON, JUICED
¼	CUP EXTRA VIRGIN OLIVE OIL

serves 4

THE CAFÉ
AT BROOKWOOD

Located 34 miles west of Downtown Houston, The Café at Brookwood is a hidden gem in the Houston area, tucked away in the city of Brookshire. The restaurant operates in conjunction with The Brookwood Community—a non-profit residential facility and vocational program for adults with disabilities, some of whom make up the staff at The Café at Brookwood. At the lunch-only restaurant, guests enjoy spectacular garden views, white-linen-topped tables and country gourmet cuisine prepared by Chef Laura Day, an alumna of the famed Culinary Institute of America in Hyde Park. Dig into plates of perfectly-breaded, romano-crusted chicken with mushroom risotto or the Argentinean beef kebobs, but save room, Chef Day's desserts are not-to-be-missed. Reservations are encouraged.

GREEN BEANS AND GUACAMOLE

NIKO TABBOULEH

3	CUPS WHOLE WHEAT ISRAELI COUSCOUS
5	CUPS CHICKEN STOCK
3	OUNCES PARSLEY, FINELY CHOPPED
1	OUNCE CHIVES, FINELY CHOPPED
½	OUNCE OREGANO, FINELY CHOPPED
½	OUNCE THYME, FINELY CHOPPED
1	OUNCE BASIL, FINELY CHOPPED
4	OUNCES CILANTRO, FINELY CHOPPED
2	TABLESPOONS GARLIC, MINCED
10	ROMA TOMATOES, SEEDED AND DICED SMALL
½	RED BELL PEPPER, DICED SMALL
½	GREEN BELL PEPPER, DICED SMALL
2	LIMES, JUICED
1	CUP OLIVE OIL
	SALT AND PEPPER

serves 8–10

In a large pot, bring 5 cups of stock to a boil. Stir in the couscous, cover and reduce heat. Simmer 8 to 10 minutes or until liquid is almost completely absorbed. Remove from heat and toss with a fork to separate. Refrigerate until ready to combine with other ingredients. In a large bowl, combine the herbs, garlic, tomatoes and peppers. Add the lime juice and olive oil. Fold in the couscous and season with salt and pepper. Serve cold or at room temperature.

NOTE: The herbs flavor the dish. Don't skimp.

GREEN BEANS AND GUACAMOLE

ORANGE BUTTER

8	OUNCES CREAM CHEESE, SOFTENED
4	OUNCES BUTTER
4	OUNCES MARGARINE
2	OUNCES POWDERED SUGAR
1	OUNCE ORANGE MARMALADE
1	TEASPOON CONFECTIONERY ORANGE PASTE, SEE NOTE
	BREAD, FOR SERVING

makes about 1 pound

In a medium bowl, combine the butter, margarine and powdered sugar with an electric mixer. Whip until fluffy. Add the cream cheese and mix on medium speed until combined. Reduce the speed to slow and add the orange marmalade and the orange paste. Refrigerate until ready to serve with your favorite bread.

NOTE: Confectionery orange paste is a food coloring and can be found among baking supplies or online.

GREEN BEANS AND GUACAMOLE

CANOPY

After establishing their Heights-set Shade, Chef Claire Smith and Russell Murrell expanded their neighborhood restaurant partnership in 2009 with Canopy—a cheerful, Montrose spot that showcases fresh, seasonally-changing cuisine. Inside, the restaurant is cheery and inviting: Oak tree photographs dot the blue-washed walls and a one-of-a-kind wooden art installation hangs overhead. The menus, created by Chef Smith, feature what she calls "global home cooking," which ranges from casual comfort foods to sophisticated selections. Choose from crowd favorites like the buttermilk-fried pork loin, pecan-crusted rainbow trout and the scallion-and-bacon-infused mac and cheese. The restaurant also boasts a well-edited wine list, creative dessert line-up and house-made artisan breads.

CRAB CAKE OVER FRIED GREEN TOMATOES

with scallion rémoulade and jalapeño chimichurri

CRAB CAKE

- ¼ CUP CELERY, DICED SMALL
- ¼ CUP RED BELL PEPPER, DICED SMALL
- ¼ CUP GREEN ONIONS, GREEN AND WHITE PARTS, CHOPPED
- ½ OUNCE FLAT LEAF PARSLEY, CHOPPED
- ½ TEASPOON FRESH THYME, CHOPPED
- 1 POUND JUMBO CRABMEAT, DRAINED AND SHELLS CLEANED
- 1 TEASPOON TABASCO SAUCE
- ½ LEMON, ZESTED AND JUICED
- 1 TABLESPOON OLD BAY SEASONING
- ⅔ CUP MAYONNAISE
- ⅓ CUP PANKO (JAPANESE BREAD CRUMBS)

  CAYENNE, SALT AND PEPPER TO TASTE

FRIED GREEN TOMATOES

- 4 GREEN TOMATOES, SLICED ½-INCH THICK
- 1½ CUPS BUTTERMILK
- ½ CUP ALL-PURPOSE FLOUR, FOR DUSTING
- 1 CUP CORN MEAL
- ½ CUP CORN FLOUR

  SALT AND PEPPER

  OIL FOR FRYING

serves 8, 3-ounce or 4, 6-ounce crab cakes

TO PREPARE THE CRAB CAKE

In a bowl, combine the mayonnaise, Old Bay Seasoning, lemon juice and Tabasco. Add the vegetables, herbs, panko and crab-meat. Gently mix together. Season crab mixture with cayenne, salt and pepper to taste. Line a sheet pan with parchment paper. Shape the crab mixture into 3-ounce patties or 6-ounce patties, placing them on the sheet pan evenly. Refrigerate until ready to cook. Crab cakes can be prepared 1 day ahead of time. Bring a non-stick sauté pan to medium heat, if using a gas stove. Heat to medium-high, if using an electric burner. Cook the crab cakes 6 to 8 minutes per side, depending on thickness, until golden brown.

TO PREPARE THE FRIED GREEN TOMATOES

Heat the frying oil to 350°F in a large, heavy skillet. Combine the corn meal and corn flour in a bowl and season with salt and pepper. Season the tomatoes with salt and pepper and lightly dust them with all-purpose flour. Pour the buttermilk into a shallow pan and dip the tomatoes in the buttermilk. Dredge the tomatoes in the corn meal and corn flour mixture, completely coating each tomato. Fry the tomatoes in the skillet in small batches, making sure not to crowd the tomatoes. Fry for 3 to 4 minutes or until golden brown.

TO PREPARE THE JALAPEÑO CHIMICHURRI

Combine all ingredients in a blender and purée.

TO PREPARE THE SCALLION RÉMOULADE

Combine first 11 ingredients in a food processor until smooth— from horseradish to olive oil. Fold in the mayonnaise and season with salt and pepper. Yields 2 cups. Store in the refrigerator.

TO SERVE

Place 3 or 4 tomatoes on each plate and top with 2, 3-ounce crab cakes or 1, 6-ounce crab cake. Drizzle the scallion rémoulade and chimichurri around the plate to taste. Top with micro greens.

NOTE: For a thicker chimichurri, reduce the olive oil to 1 cup.

JALAPEÑO CHIMICHURRI

- 6 JALAPEÑOS, SEEDED
- 1 CUP FLAT LEAF PARSLEY, LEAVES ONLY
- 1 TABLESPOON LEMON JUICE
- ¼ TEASPOON KOSHER SALT
- 2 CUPS OLIVE OIL

  DASH OF CRUSHED RED PEPPER

SCALLION RÉMOULADE

- 1 TABLESPOON HORSERADISH
- 1 TABLESPOON WHOLE GRAIN MUSTARD
- ½ LEMON, JUICED
- ½ TEASPOON TABASCO SAUCE
- 1 TEASPOON WORCESTERSHIRE SAUCE

  DASH CAYENNE

- ½ TEASPOON GRANULATED SUGAR
- ½ CUP SCALLIONS, CHOPPED
- ½ CUP CELERY, CHOPPED
- 1 JALAPEÑO, SEEDED AND CHOPPED
- 1 TABLESPOON OLIVE OIL
- ½ CUP MAYONNAISE

  SALT AND PEPPER

  MICRO GREENS, FOR GARNISH

CARRABBA'S

Carrabba's is a home away from home for many Houstonians, who are as comfortable sitting at the bar, as they are in their own living room. Founded by Johnny Carrabba and his uncle Damian Mandola, the Italian restaurant has blossomed into a national chain in its more than 25-year history. Today, the original location on Kirby Drive remains locally-owned, still serving up Sicilian-inspired dishes based on old family recipes. The menu mixes signature, house-made pastas, salads and meat dishes roasted in the wood-burning grill. Fan favorites include the pollo Rosa Maria and the Chicken Bryan, the latter of which is topped with goat cheese, sundried tomatoes and a basil-lemon butter sauce.

GREEN BEANS

Preheat the oven to 350°F.

TO PREPARE THE MOIST YELLOW CAKE

Spray a 2½-inch deep, 9 x 11 inch cake pan with non-stick spray. In a large bowl, sift together the flour, baking powder and baking soda. Set aside. In another large bowl, cream together the butter and sugar until light and fluffy. Beat in the eggs one at a time, then stir in the vanilla. Beat in the flour mixture alternately with the buttermilk, mixing until just incorporated. Pour batter into prepared pan. Bake in a conventional, not convection, oven for 30 to 35 minutes or until a toothpick, inserted in the center of the cake, comes out clean. Let cake cool.

TO ASSEMBLE THE CAKE AND TOPPING

After the cake has cooled, poke holes throughout cake with a skewer, making 4 holes across and 6 holes down. This will allow the juices from the pineapple and strawberries to seep into the cake. Spread the pineapple over the cake. Lay strawberries and then bananas over the pineapple. Spread pudding over bananas. Cover the cake with Cool Whip, smoothing the Cool Whip with a spatula to make sure no pudding shows through. Cover the cake with a dome lid and refrigerate for 3 hours.

NOTE: Use a slotted spoon when topping the cake with the pineapple and the strawberries to allow some juice to be transferred, but not so much that it makes the cake overly soggy.

CAKE

1	CUP BUTTER
2½	CUPS WHITE SUGAR
3	EGGS
1½	TEASPOONS VANILLA EXTRACT
2½	CUPS BUTTERMILK
3¾	CUPS ALL-PURPOSE FLOUR
2¼	TEASPOONS BAKING POWDER
2½	TEASPOONS BAKING SODA

TOPPING

20	WEIGHT OUNCES PREPARED SWEETENED CRUSHED PINEAPPLE
2	10-OUNCE PACKAGES BIRDSEYE FROZEN STRAWBERRIES
4	BANANAS, SLICED INTO ¼ INCH THICK ROUNDS
24	WEIGHT OUNCES VANILLA PUDDING, PREPARED ACCORDING TO PACKAGE
8	WEIGHT OUNCES COOL WHIP

serves 12

GREEN BEANS AND GUACAMOLE

CONCHIGLIE PICCHI PACCHIU

CARRABBA'S

4	CUPS CANNED PLUM TOMATOES, SEEDED AND PEELED
¾	CUP EXTRA VIRGIN OLIVE OIL
8	CLOVES GARLIC, THINLY SLICED
1	TABLESPOON KOSHER SALT
1	TABLESPOON FRESHLY-GROUND BLACK PEPPER
12	BASIL LEAVES, COARSELY CHOPPED
1	POUND SEASHELL PASTA

serves 4–6

Place tomatoes, with their juices, in a large stainless bowl. Crush tomatoes as small as possible with your hands. Place the garlic and ½ cup of the extra virgin olive oil into a saucepan over low heat. Cook until garlic softens and releases flavor into the oil. Do not allow to brown. Add garlic and oil mixture to the tomato mixture along with the remaining ¼ cup of oil. Season with salt and pepper. Stir until thoroughly combined. Add the basil and stir until all ingredients are thoroughly mixed. Meanwhile, cook 1 pound of seashell pasta for 13 minutes. Drain and then add to hot Picchi Pacchiu sauce.

GREEN BEANS AND GUACAMOLE

CIAO BELLO

Legendary Houston restaurateur Tony Vallone teamed up with son, Jeff, for the 2009 opening of their casual Italian outpost—Ciao Bello. The Tanglewood-set venture draws neighboring families for *cucina casalinga*—home cooking—served in a light and bright setting. Inside, abstract murals by John Ross Palmer add to the lively design and help brighten the space, including Ciao Bello's air-conditioned, glass-door-enclosed patio. Guests can choose from an array of seafood, pizza and handmade pasta dishes that fill the always-changing menu. Family favorites like spaghetti & meatballs and lasagna Bolognese live alongside more daring options like the white wine-and-tomato-imbued mussels Aiello and the rabbit cacciatore.

GREEN BEANS AND GUACAM

ORECCHIETTE
with Italian sausage, rapini and Italian breadcrumbs

2	CUPS ORECCHIETTE, COOKED AL DENTE
1	CUP RAPINI FLORETS, BLANCHED
	PINCH FENNEL SEED
1	CUP ITALIAN SAUSAGE, CASINGS REMOVED
2	TABLESPOONS BUTTER
2	ANCHOVY FILLETS
2	TEASPOONS GARLIC
1	CUP PECORINO ROMANO OR PARMESAN, FRESHLY GRATED
2	TABLESPOONS EXTRA VIRGIN OLIVE OIL
	PINCH RED CHILI FLAKES
4	TABLESPOONS ITALIAN BREADCRUMBS

serves 2

In a heavy-bottom sauté pan, add olive oil, garlic, fennel and anchovy. Use a spoon to crush the anchovy fillets into a paste as it cooks. Add sausage and brown slightly, breaking it into small pieces. Add a pinch of red chili flakes, the rapini florets and butter. Remove from the heat and add pasta and cheese. Toss lightly to melt cheese. Plate the pasta. Top with bread-crumbs and another small pinch of chili flakes.

GREEN BEANS AND GUACAMOLE

PARMESAN CRUSTED ALASKAN HALIBUT
with stewed lentils and Texas blue crab

CIAO BELLO

4   HALIBUT FILLETS, ABOUT 6 OUNCES EACH

1   CUP TEXAS BLUE CRAB

CRUST

1   CUP PARMESAN, GRATED

½   CUP BREAD CRUMBS, PLAIN

½   CUP BUTTER, CUBED AND SOFTENED

2   TABLESPOONS PARSLEY, CHOPPED

LENTILS

1   CUP LENTILS

½   CUP CARROTS, DICED SMALL

½   CUP SHALLOTS, SLICED

2   CUPS CHICKEN BROTH

    SHERRY VINEGAR

1   TABLESPOON BUTTER

serves 4

Preheat oven to 425°F.

TO PREPARE THE CRUST
Mix all of the ingredients by hand and
apply a thin layer over the top of the fish.
Place fish in a baking pan.

TO PREPARE THE LENTILS
Cook the lentils and carrots in the chicken
broth, over medium heat, until tender.
Remove from heat and add shallots, butter and a dash of Sherry vinegar. Set aside
and keep warm.

TO PREPARE THE HALIBUT
Bake the crusted fish in the oven with a
bit of chicken stock in bottom of the pan,
about 8 to 10 minutes. Remove the fillets
from the pan, when done, and keep warm.
Add the crab to the pan with the butter to
make a sauce.

TO SERVE
Ladle lentils into shallow bowls. Place
halibut fillets on top. Spoon crab sauce
over each fillet.

SMALL PLATES

spicy fennel sausage			
whipped mortadella	10		
crispy globe artichoke	10		
octopus carpaccio	9		
brick oven sardines	11		
fritto misto	13	burrata	13
meatball al forno	10	tuna crudo	13
bruschette e giare	18	pane campagnola	9
salumi board	17		

PIZZA

the marinara	12	the margherita	14
the neapolitan	15	the bianca	15
Italian sausage	17	mushrooms	16
coppa "ham & eggs"	17	lamb sausage	16
summer squash	14	potato	13

PASTA

spaghetti carbonara			18
mafalda & meatballs			18
foglie di carciofo			17
agnolotti	17	lasagne	19
capellini	15	ravioli	16
cicones	17	linguine	18
gnocchi	17		

COPPA
RISTORANTE ITALIANO

COPPA
RISTORANTE ITALIANO

Restaurateurs Grant Cooper and Charles Clark—of Ibiza and Brasserie 19 fame—have unveiled a new venture, Coppa Ristorante Italiano, which opened in late-summer 2011. Located in the stylish space that was most recently home to Cooper and Clark's Catalan restaurant, Coppa has welcomed an abbreviated facelift, which included the addition of rustic accents, funky chandeliers and a wood-burning oven. In her new role, Chef Brandi Key created an Italian-American menu that highlights the restaurant's signature Neopolitan pizza, seafood dishes and pasta plates. Go for favorites like the piping-hot lasagne, the egg-topped spaghetti carbonara or one of the perfectly-charred pizzas, paired with a selection from the well-priced wine list.

GREEN BEANS AND GUACAMOLE

PESCE EN CARTUCCIO

COPPA

4   SNAPPER FILLETS, SKINLESS, BONELESS,
    APPROXIMATELY 8 OUNCES EACH

    OLIVE OIL, AS NEEDED

    KOSHER SALT, AS NEEDED

    BLACK PEPPER, AS NEEDED

8   LEMON SLICES

8   BASIL LEAVES

4   OREGANO SPRIGS

4   TABLESPOONS BUTTER, DICED SMALL

    PARCHMENT PAPER

    PAPER CLIPS

serves 4

Preheat oven to 400°F.

Season each fillet evenly with olive oil, kosher salt and black pepper. Set aside. With scissors, cut 4, 14-inch by 14-inch squares of parchment paper. Place one seasoned fish fillet on the left side of each piece of parchment, leaving a 1-inch margin of parchment visible around the fish. Divide the lemon slices, basil leaves, oregano and diced butter among all 4 pieces of fish, arranging neatly on top. Fold the right side of one of the parchment pieces, so that it meets the left edge of the paper, covering the fish.

Working with one edge at a time, make several ¼ inch folds along the 3 edges to seal the fish inside of the paper. If needed, secure the corners with paper clips to ensure the packet is well-sealed. Repeat this process for the remaining fish fillets. Place the parchment-wrapped packets on baking sheet and bake for 12 to 15 minutes, or until the fish are just cooked through. Remove the packets from the oven and discard the paper clips. Using scissors, cut open each packet and drizzle olive oil over each fillet. Serve immediately in the parchment paper.

NOTE: If you are concerned if the fish is done, remove one of the packets from the oven and carefully open one of the corners. Be cautious, as steam will escape the packet and could cause a burn. Check the fish with a fork to see if it is cooked. If more time is needed, close the corner of the packet and continue baking.

ZEPPOLE
COPPA

4 QUARTS CANOLA OIL

1 CUP ALL-PURPOSE FLOUR

1 TEASPOON BAKING POWDER

1 TABLESPOON SUGAR

PINCH OF SALT

½ CUP RICOTTA CHEESE

2 WHOLE EGGS

POWDERED SUGAR, AS NEEDED

serves 6

Heat canola oil in an 8-quart Dutch oven until the temperature reaches 350°F. While the oil is heating, mix flour, baking powder, sugar and salt in a mixing bowl with a wire whisk. In a separate bowl, mix ricotta and whole eggs with a wire whisk, making sure that the mixture is completely smooth, before adding to the flour mixture. Whisk until just combined. Batter will be lumpy. Using 2 large spoons, place 2 tablespoons of batter at a time into the hot oil. The batter will sink to the bottom of the oil, floating to the top after a few seconds. Should the batter stick to the bottom of the Dutch oven, carefully loosen the batter. Fry each zeppole for 3 to 4 minutes, turning occasionally to ensure even browning and thorough cooking. Fry as many as 8 zeppole at a time, but be careful not to crowd them. Line a plate with paper towels. Using a skimmer, remove zeppole from the oil and transfer to paper towels to drain. Fry remaining batter, then sift a generous amount of powdered sugar on top until completely coated. Serve immediately.

NOTE: Zeppole pairs well with chocolate sauce or Nutella.

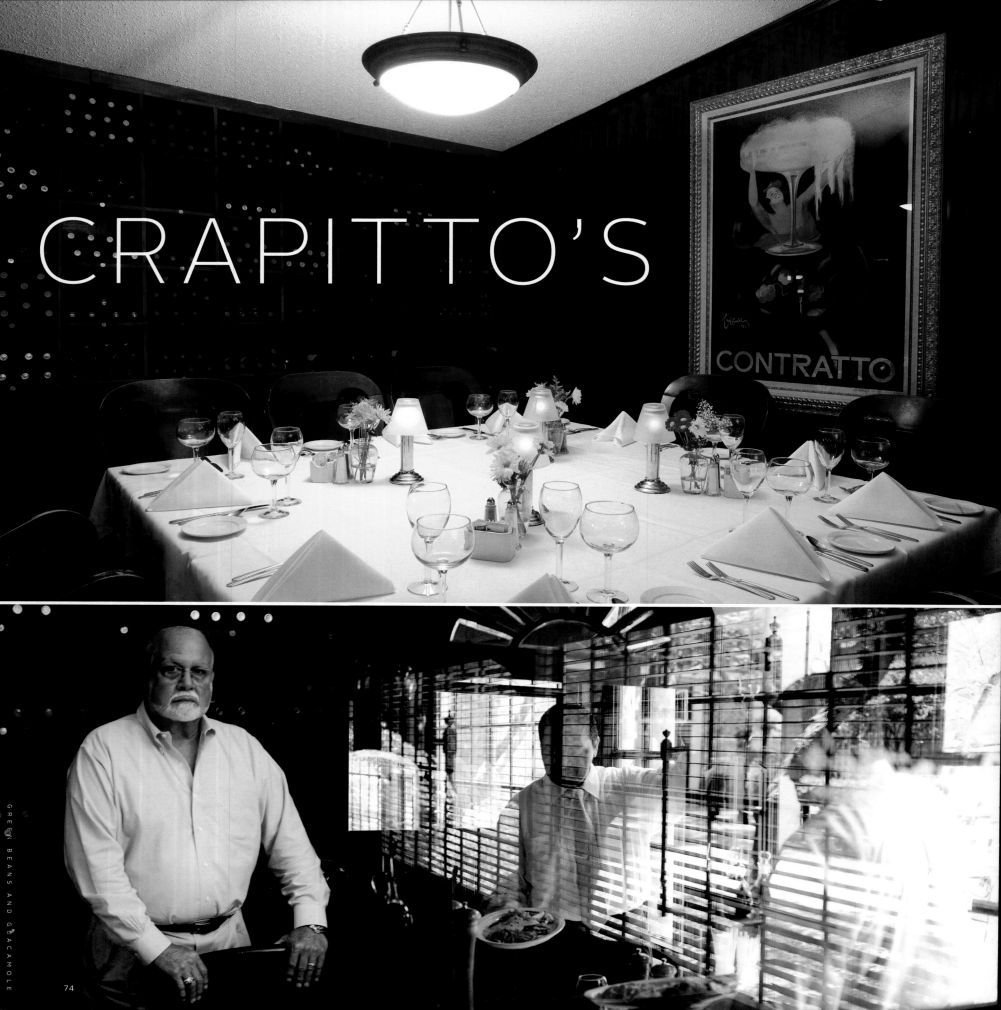

CRAPITTO'S

GREEN BEANS AND GUACAMOLE

Crapitto's Cucina Italiana's converted farmhouse space sits quietly under 100-year-old oak trees, in the shadow of the Galleria and just inside the bustling 610 Loop. Part of one of Houston's oldest Italian families, Frank Crapitto delivers dishes made from age-old family recipes and locally-sourced produce, beef, lamb and seafood. Frank even grows his own tomatoes in Huntsville, which he sells during high-yielding seasons. Crapitto's food is unfailing, too, with an array of pasta, chicken and fish items. The signature grilled veal chop, topped with a Roquefort butter sauce, remains a standout, as do the restaurant's desserts. The famous cheesecake, tiramisu and spumoni ice cream are all solid selections. On nice Houston days, Crapitto's patio is hard to beat for lunch or dinner.

GREEN BEANS AND GUACAMOLE

GRAPITTO'S

CHICKEN

1 CLOVE GARLIC, FINELY CHOPPED

1 TABLESPOON DIJON MUSTARD

3 TABLESPOONS OLIVE OIL, DIVIDED

1 TABLESPOON ROSEMARY, CHOPPED

2 8-OUNCE CHICKEN BREAST HALVES, POUNDED TO ½-INCH THICKNESS

SALT AND GROUND BLACK PEPPER

SAUCE

¼ CUP WHITE WINE

¼ CUP CHICKEN BROTH

1 TABLESPOON DIJON MUSTARD

1 TABLESPOON CAPERS, DRAINED

¼ CUP WHIPPING CREAM

serves 2

TO MARINATE THE CHICKEN
In a bowl, combine garlic, 1 tablespoon mustard, 1 tablespoon olive oil and rosemary to make a marinade. Season chicken with salt and pepper, then place in marinade and refrigerate in a glass container or plastic bag for a minimum of 2 hours or preferably overnight.

TO PREPARE THE CHICKEN
Heat remaining 2 tablespoons olive oil over medium-high heat and sauté chicken, turning several times until browned on both sides. Do not overcook. Set aside on a serving dish.

TO PREPARE THE SAUCE
Place sauté pan over medium-high heat and add wine, broth, capers and cream. Heat until reduced and thickened, 6 to 7 minutes. Stir in remaining 1 tablespoon mustard and then return the chicken to the pan. When chicken is heated through, transfer to plates and spoon sauce over chicken.

GREEN BEANS AND GUACAMOLE

BLACKENED SALMON SALAD

CRAPITTO'S

SALMON

4   6-OUNCE SALMON FILLETS

2   TABLESPOONS OLIVE OIL

SEASONING

1½   TABLESPOONS THYME

1   TEASPOON ONION POWDER

1   TEASPOON GARLIC POWDER, GRANULATED

½   TEASPOON PAPRIKA

½   TEASPOON CAYENNE

½   TEASPOON KOSHER SALT

½   TEASPOON BLACK PEPPER

SALAD

3   CUPS MIXED GREENS

½   CUP TOMATO, DICED

½   CUP AVOCADO, PEELED, SEEDED AND DICED

¼   CUP RED ONION, CHOPPED

1   TABLESPOON CILANTRO, CHOPPED

    JUICE OF 1 LIME

¼   CUP EXTRA VIRGIN OLIVE OIL

    SALT AND PEPPER

serves 4

Preheat oven to 400°F.

TO PREPARE THE SEASONING
Combine all seasoning ingredients in a
bowl and mix well.

TO PREPARE THE SALMON
Coat salmon in olive oil and dredge in
seasoning mixture. Lightly coat a large
sauté pan with olive oil and sear fish for
1 minute on each side, over medium-high
heat. Transfer to oven and finish cooking
5 to 10 minutes to desired doneness.

TO PREPARE THE SALAD
Toss all salad ingredients in a bowl.

TO SERVE
Divide salad among 4 plates and top each
with a salmon fillet.

GREEN BEANS AND GUACAMOLE

CULLEN'S
UPSCALE AMERICAN GRILLE

GREEN BEANS AND GUACAMOLE

Located in Clear Lake, Cullen's Upscale American Grille is more than a restaurant, it's a dining destination. Chef Paul Lewis—an alum of the Four Seasons—sends out an array of in-house dry-aged meats, fresh catch and locally-grown produce dishes, but the bone-in rib eye and wasabi-glazed mahi-mahi aren't the only reasons guests venture beyond the Beltway. In addition to an elegant dining space and casual grill option, Cullen's opulent 30,000-square-foot facility houses an event-ready ballroom, seven private dining rooms, patio seating and a live entertainment venue—but for supreme seclusion, the Macy's Table can't be beat. The 12-person, glass-encased dining space is suspended high above the main dining room, affording guests a dramatic, bird's-eye view

PROSCIUTTO-WRAPPED CHICKEN BREAST
with heirloom grits and braised greens

PROSCIUTTO-WRAPPED CHICKEN

4	CHICKEN BREASTS
1	TABLESPOON EXTRA VIRGIN OLIVE OIL
4	OUNCES CHEVRE GOAT CHEESE
4	OUNCES PROSCIUTTO, SLICED THIN
2	CUPS BRAISED GREENS, SEE RECIPE
3	CUPS SOFT GRITS, SEE RECIPE
½	CUP LEMON THYME JUS, SEE RECIPE AND NOTE
	SALT AND PEPPER
4	THYME SPRIGS, FOR GARNISH

SOFT GRITS

1½	CUPS ANSON MILLS GRITS, SEE NOTE
4½	CUPS WATER
1	TABLESPOON BUTTER, DICED
	SALT

serves 2

Preheat oven to 450°F.

TO PREPARE THE GRITS:
Combine the grits and water in a pot over low heat. Stir constantly until soft, about 40 to 45 minutes. Remove from heat and add butter. Season with salt.

TO PREPARE THE GREENS:
Render the pancetta in a pan. Add onion and garlic and sauté until tender, about 2 minutes. Add chicken stock to deglaze the pan, scraping any bits from bottom or sides. Add the mustard greens and cook until wilted. Reduce heat, cover and simmer for about 1 hour or until tender. Remove from heat. Add the vinegar and season with salt and pepper.

TO PREPARE THE JUS:
Place the lemon thyme in a large bowl. Heat the olive oil in a large pot over medium-high heat. Add the onions, carrots, leeks and garlic. Caramelize vegetables, stirring often. Add the tomato purée, stirring until it begins to brown and caramelize. Add the wine and reduce until almost dry. Add the veal stock, oxtails, thyme, rosemary and peppercorns. Bring to a boil and then reduce heat. Simmer until reduced by half, skimming constantly. Remove from heat. Strain through a sieve, over the lemon thyme, into the bowl. Infuse for 30 minutes. Strain again. Set aside.

TO PREPARE THE CHICKEN:
Cut a slit into the side of the thickest part of each chicken breast. Stuff each breast with 1 ounce of goat cheese and then wrap with prosciutto. Heat olive oil in a sauté pan until smoking. Sear chicken breasts on both sides and then finish cooking in the preheated oven.

TO SERVE:
For each serving, ladle ¾ cup of grits into a wide shallow bowl. Spoon ½ cup of braised greens over grits and top with chicken breast. Spoon lemon thyme jus over dish and garnish with thyme sprig.

NOTE: To prepare this recipe, as indicated, requires significant time. Substitutions can be made for the chicken and veal stocks. If short on time, see Appendix for a modified lemon thyme jus recipe. Use any good quality grits or substitute with instant, following package directions.

BRAISED GREENS

¾	BUNCH MUSTARD GREENS, PICKED, WASHED THOROUGHLY, FREE OF GRIT
1	OUNCE PANCETTA, CUT INTO SMALL STRIPS
⅛	CUP YELLOW ONIONS, FINELY CHOPPED
1	TABLESPOON GARLIC, SLICED
¾	CUP CHICKEN STOCK
½	CUP APPLE CIDER VINEGAR
	SALT AND PEPPER

LEMON THYME JUS

3	OUNCES OXTAILS, CHOPPED AND ROASTED AT 400°F UNTIL GOLDEN
1	OUNCE EXTRA VIRGIN OLIVE OIL
1	YELLOW ONION, CHOPPED
3	OUNCES CARROTS, PEELED AND CHOPPED
¼	BUNCH LEEKS, CHOPPED AND WASHED
1	OUNCE GARLIC
½	TABLESPOON TOMATO PURÉE
½	GALLON VEAL STOCK
100	MILLILITERS RED WINE
1	SPRIG THYME
1	SPRIG ROSEMARY
½	TEASPOON BLACK PEPPERCORNS
1½	OUNCES LEMON THYME, STEMMED

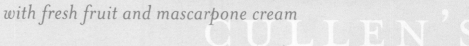

1	PACKAGE OF PHYLLO DOUGH, THAWED, CUT INTO 4 SQUARES
6	OUNCES BUTTER, MELTED
6	OUNCES CINNAMON SUGAR
1	500-GRAM TUB ITALIAN MASCARPONE CHEESE
1	CUP HEAVY WHIPPING CREAM
¼	CUP POWDERED SUGAR
1	TEASPOON VANILLA EXTRACT
3	CUPS FRESH SUMMER FRUIT SUCH AS PEACHES, APRICOTS, CHERRIES, RASPBERRIES AND BLUEBERRIES, WASHED AND CUT
½	TABLESPOON SUGAR

serves 6–8

Preheat oven to 350°F.

Spray a large muffin tin with non-stick spray. Using 5 pieces of phyllo for each cup, place 1 square on the work surface. Cover remaining phyllo with plastic wrap and a damp towel to prevent from drying. Brush first layer lightly with melted butter. Sprinkle with cinnamon sugar. Place next square slightly off center from the first one, turning to achieve a star pattern. Brush with butter and sprinkle with cinnamon sugar. Repeat 3 more times, making a stack of 5 squares.

Lift phyllo stack from work surface and press into sprayed muffin cup. Repeat procedure 5 more times, making at least 6 to 8 phyllo cups. Bake phyllo cups until golden brown, about 9 to 12 minutes. Lift phyllo cups from pan and place on rack to cool completely.

Place fruit in a bowl and sprinkle with sugar to draw out juice. In a stand mixer, using the whip attachment, combine the whipping cream and vanilla extract. Whip on medium speed until soft peaks form. Place mascarpone in a bowl large enough to hold both whipped cream and cheese. Sift powdered sugar over cheese. Mix together with a spatula until smooth. Add ¼ of the whipped cream and fold until smooth. Add remaining cream and fold together until smooth. Spoon mascarpone cream into the phyllo cups. Top with fresh fruit and dust with powdered sugar.

NOTE: As an alternative to purchased cinnamon sugar, combine ½ cup sugar with 1 tablespoon cinnamon. Increase cinnamon to desired taste. Leftover phyllo dough can be wrapped and refrigerated for later use.

GREEN BEANS AND GUACAMOLE

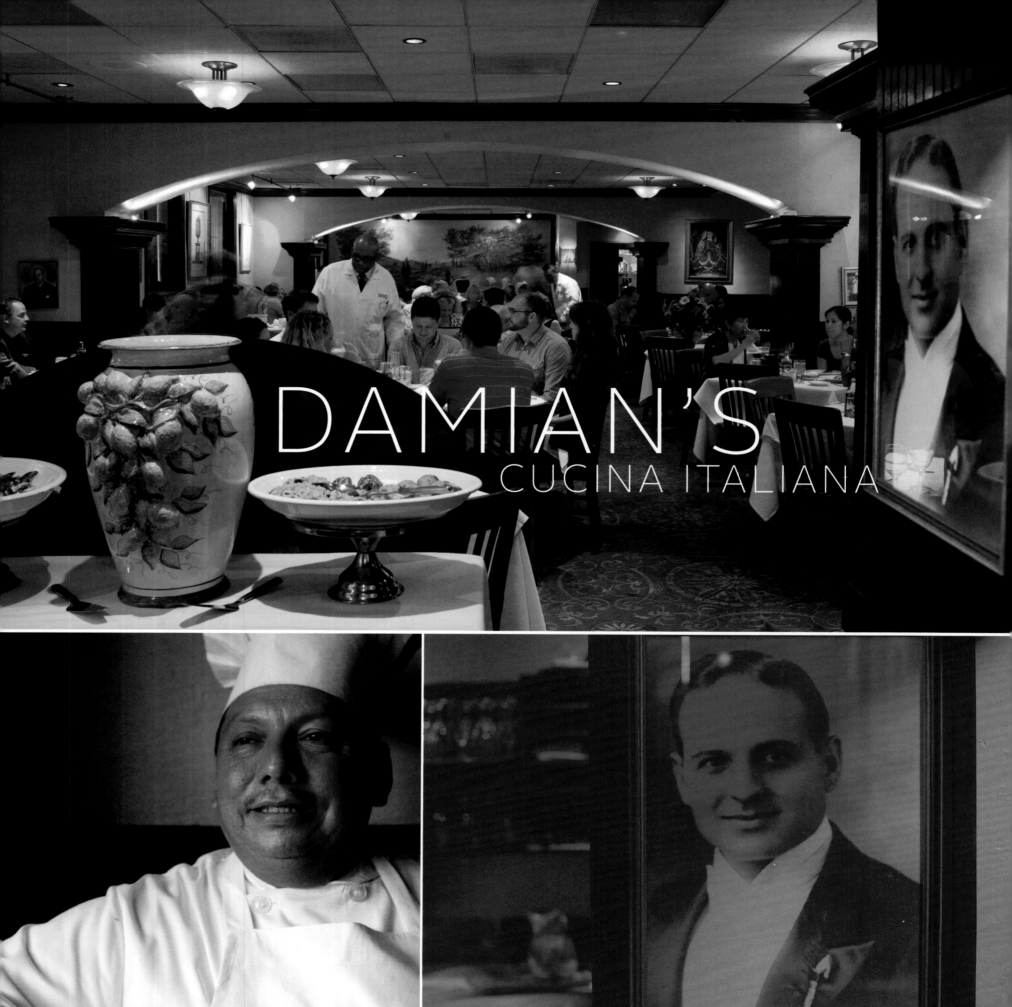

DAMIAN'S
CUCINA ITALIANA

Impeccable service and authentic Italian fare are trademarks of Midtown's Damian's Cucina Italiana. Originally founded by restaurateur Damian Mandola—of Carrabba's and D'amico's fame—the local fixture has been owned and operated by his cousins, Joseph 'Bubba' Butera and Frankie Mandola, since 1992. Easily accessible from Downtown, Damian's draws a loyal lunch crowd, where many a business lunch has been enjoyed, along with post-work get-togethers. Inside, vaulted archways, vintage family photos and a pastoral mural spanning the back wall, lend to Damian's old-world atmosphere. The kitchen sends out a variety of homemade pasta, antipasto and salad dishes, along with fresh-baked breads and desserts, all of which are perfectly complemented by one of the restaurant's many wine options.

GREEN BEANS AND GUACAMOLE

Preheat the oven to 350°F.

TO PREPARE CROUTONS:
Toss bread with olive oil. Season with salt and pepper. Spread in a single layer on a rimmed baking sheet. Bake for 20 to 30 minutes or until golden brown, turning to brown all sides.

TO PREPARE THE SALAD:
In a large wooden bowl, sprinkle salt and add 1 teaspoon of olive oil. Swirl 1 garlic clove in the oil with a fork and coat the wall of the bowl with the olive oil and the juice of the garlic. Mash the garlic clove into the olive oil to form a paste. Add anchovy and mash it with the fork to combine with the garlic paste and form a smooth consistency. Add the dry mustard, red wine vinegar, Worcestershire sauce and a squeeze from the lemon. Thoroughly combine with the garlic-anchovy mixture. Add 2 teaspoons olive oil and egg yolk with a little bit of egg white. Mix thoroughly until smooth and creamy. Add 1 tablespoon of Parmesan and mix well. Add the romaine and toss until the dressing coats the lettuce. Sprinkle a little more Parmesan over the romaine. Season with pepper. Toss lightly, add croutons and toss a few more times. Croutons should not become soggy. Serve on chilled dinner plates. Sprinkle with additional Parmesan and pepper.

CROUTONS

2	CUPS BREAD, CRUST REMOVED AND CUBED
1½	TABLESPOONS OLIVE OIL
	SALT AND PEPPER

SALAD

	PINCH OF SALT
1	GARLIC CLOVE
¼	TEASPOON DRY MUSTARD
½	LEMON
1	EGG
3	TABLESPOONS PARMESAN CHEESE, GRATED
	FRESHLY-GROUND BLACK PEPPER
3	TEASPOONS OLIVE OIL
1-2	ANCHOVIES
1	TEASPOON RED WINE VINEGAR
1	TEASPOON WORCESTERSHIRE SAUCE
1-2	HEADS OF ROMAINE LETTUCE, ENOUGH FOR 2, INNER LEAVES ONLY, WASHED, DRIED AND TORN INTO PIECES

serves 2

GREEN BEANS AND GUACAMOLE

SPAGHETTI ALLA CARBONARA

DAMIAN'S

6½ OUNCES OF SPAGHETTI

2 OUNCES OLIVE OIL

4 TABLESPOONS PANCETTA, DICED

2 TABLESPOONS SCALLIONS, SLICED

1 TEASPOON GARLIC, CHOPPED

4 OUNCES HEAVY CREAM

2 EGG YOLKS

2 OUNCES PARMESAN, GRATED

SALT AND PEPPER

serves 2

In a medium skillet, heat pancetta and olive oil over a medium-low flame and cook until it begins to brown. Add the scallions and garlic, cook 1 to 2 more minutes. The pancetta should be crispy. Remove from heat and add the heavy cream, salt and pepper. In a large bowl, beat the eggs and Parmesan and set aside. Bring a pot of lightly-salted water to a boil. Add spaghetti and cook until al dente. Drain and toss pasta with the pancetta-cream mixture. Quickly transfer the pasta to the egg and cheese mixture. Toss to coat and serve immediately.

FEAST

Nose-to-tail cooking finds a loyal fan base and home at Montrose's Feast. Since opening in 2008, the boundary-pushing endeavor has welcomed rave reviews from *Bon Appetit*, *GQ* magazine and even a nomination for Best New Restaurant by the James Beard Foundation. Rustic charm abounds at the British-leaning restaurant, where hardwood floors and soft lighting set the scene for epicurean adventures filled with braised beef tongue and pig's head terrine. Of course, there's more to the restaurant's weekly-changing menu than offal cooking, too. Diners looking to play it safe will appreciate the sea scallops, smoked salmon and the Spanish-style meatballs in a spicy tomato sauce.

BITTER ORANGE TART

4 TABLESPOONS BUTTER

4 TABLESPOONS BROWN SUGAR

1 LARGE ORANGE, SLICED INTO THIN ROUNDS

1 SHEET PUFF PASTRY, ROLLED THIN,
CUT INTO A 10-INCH ROUND

CLOTTED OR REGULAR CREAM,
FOR SERVING

CONFECTIONERS' SUGAR, FOR DUSTING

serves 6

Preheat oven to 350°F.

Line the bottom of a 10-inch pie dish with dampened parchment paper. In a bowl, cream butter and sugar and then spread over the parchment paper. Chill in the refrigerator for 30 minutes. Remove from refrigerator and place orange slices on the butter and sugar base, overlapping slightly. Cover with puff pastry and prick the surface with a fork. Bake for 30 minutes. Remove from oven and turn out onto a serving dish. Remove the parchment paper. Serve with clotted or regular cream and dust with confectioners' sugar.

FRANK'S CHOP HOUSE

Founded by Frank Crapitto—of the Highland Village-area's Crapitto's Cucina Italiana—brings his commitment to locally-sourced products and a casual dining atmosphere to River Oaks' Frank's Chop House. The neighborhood steakhouse, which opened in 2008, is clubby, outfitted in dark-wood tones, soft lighting and an exposed-beam ceiling—an inviting respite for locals craving upscale comfort food. Open for lunch and dinner, regulars at Frank's return for the popular chicken fried steak, paired with mashed potatoes, roasted vegetables and cracked-pepper cream gravy. The Gulf shrimp BLT and maple-brined, double-bone pork chop are also crowd favorites. Oenophiles will appreciate the restaurant's 110-bottle international wine list.

BRAISED SHORT RIBS
with soft polenta

RIBS

6	BONE-IN SHORT RIBS, ABOUT 5¾ POUNDS
	KOSHER SALT, AS NEEDED
	EXTRA VIRGIN OLIVE OIL, AS NEEDED
1	LARGE SPANISH ONION, CUT INTO ½-INCH PIECES
2	RIBS OF CELERY, CUT INTO ½-INCH PIECES
2	CARROTS, PEELED, CUT IN HALF LENGTHWISE AND CUT INTO ½-INCH PIECES
1½	CUPS TOMATO PASTE
2-3	CUPS HEARTY RED WINE, SUCH AS BAROLO
2	CUPS FRESH, DARK CHICKEN STOCK OR WATER
1	BUNCH FRESH THYME, TIED WITH KITCHEN STRING
2	BAY LEAVES

POLENTA

4	CUPS WATER
1	CUP POLENTA
1	TEASPOON SALT
3	TABLESPOONS BUTTER
½	CUP PARMESAN, GRATED

serves 4-6

Preheat oven to 375°F.

TO PREPARE THE RIBS

Trim the excess fat from each short rib and season generously with salt and freshly-ground black pepper, a day in advance, if possible. In a heavy-bottom pot, large enough to accommodate all the meat and vegetables, coat the bottom with olive oil and bring to a high heat. Add the short ribs to the pan and lower the heat to medium. Brown both sides, about 2 to 3 minutes per side. Do not overcrowd the pan, as they will steam. Cook in batches, if necessary. Remove the ribs from the pan and drain off the excess oil. Increase the heat to medium-high and add the tomato paste. Toast for 4 minutes. Add the onions and sauté for 3 minutes, then add the remainder of the vegetables. Be sure to scrape up the entire bottom of the pan with a wooden spoon as the vegetables release their liquid.

Deglaze the pan with the wine and, when all the bits are scraped up, return the short ribs back to the pot and add the stock until it covers the top of the short ribs. Add the fresh thyme and bay leaves. Cover the pot and place in the oven for 3 hours. Check periodically during the cooking process to add more stock, if needed. When done, the meat should be very tender, but not falling apart. The braising liquid may be reduced after removing the short ribs and then puréed in a food mill. Serve over soft polenta with lots of the braising juices.

TO PREPARE THE POLENTA

Heat the water in a heavy-bottomed pot until boiling. Whisk in the polenta and salt. Stir until the polenta is suspended in the water and no longer settles to the bottom of the pot. Cook for 1 hour, stirring occasionally, at a bare simmer. Add water if it gets too thick. Remove from heat. Add butter and Parmesan.

TO SERVE

Ladle polenta onto plates, top with short ribs and pan juices.

Preheat oven to 375°F.

TO PREPARE THE CRUST

In a bowl, combine the cracker crumbs, nuts and cinnamon. Stir in the butter. Press the crust mixture into the bottom and up the sides of a 9-inch springform pan.

TO PREPARE THE FILLING

In a mixing bowl, combine cream cheese, sugar, cornstarch and vanilla. Beat until fluffy. Add eggs and yolks all at once, beating on low speed, until just combined. Fold in the cream and the pumpkin purée. It will appear broken, but will bake beautifully. Pour into the crust-lined pan. Place on a shallow baking pan in oven. Bake for 35 to 40 minutes or until the center appears nearly set when shaken. Cool 15 minutes. Loosen sides of the pan and cool for 30 minutes. Chill for 4 hours before serving. Decorate with sugared pumpkin seeds and serve with caramel sauce.

NOTE: For sugared pumpkin seeds, prepare as follows: 1 cup pumpkins seeds, 1 tablespoon butter, 1 tablespoon sugar (sprinkling of nutmeg or cinnamon, if desired). Rinse pumpkin seeds and pat dry. Toss with butter, sugar and spices (if using). Spread on a lightly-greased baking sheet at 300°F for 45 to 60 minutes until golden and crunchy, stirring occasionally. Cheesecake can be served with fresh fruit, as an alternative.

CRUST

1¾	CUPS GRAHAM CRACKER CRUMBS
¼	CUP PECANS, FINELY GROUND
½	TEASPOON GROUND CINNAMON
½	CUP UNSALTED BUTTER, MELTED

FILLING

3	PACKAGES CREAM CHEESE (8 OUNCES EACH), SOFTENED
1½	CUPS SUGAR
2	TABLESPOONS CORNSTARCH
1	TEASPOON VANILLA
2	EGGS
2	EGG YOLKS
¼	CUP HEAVY CREAM
1	CAN PUMPKIN PURÉE (14 OUNCES)
	SUGARED PUMPKIN SEEDS, SEE NOTE
¼	CUP CARAMEL SAUCE
	POWDERED SUGAR

serves 8

GREEN BEANS AND GUACAMOLE

GIGI'S
ASIAN BISTRO & DUMPLING BAR

East meets west inside the Galleria's Gigi's Asian Bistro & Dumpling Bar. Set on the street level of the shopping complex, restaurateur Gigi Huang's concept reflects an oriental collage of Chinese, Thai, Vietnamese, Malaysian and Singaporean dishes. A cascade of 15,000 silk cherry blossoms form an eye-catching canopy above the main dining room—one of four, well-designed interior spaces. While Gigi's is most popular during its all-you-can-eat dim sum, served on Saturday and Sunday, it's also a great lunch and dinner stop, as well as a welcome respite between shopping sprees. The pad Thai, green curry chicken and the heavenly beef are all savory selections, as is the Return of the Phoenix—a favorite culled from the Huang family's sorely-missed Hunan restaurant.

SHAKING BEEF
with chili–lime vinaigrette
GIGI'S

VINAIGRETTE

5 THAI CHILI PIECES, GROUND OR MINCED

2 OUNCES LIME JUICE

4 OUNCES FISH SAUCE,
PREFERABLY THREE CRABS BRAND

1 OUNCE PALM SUGAR, CHOPPED INTO
SMALL CHUNKS

2 TEASPOONS CILANTRO, CHOPPED

½ TEASPOON GARLIC, CHOPPED

BEEF

VEGETABLE OIL FOR WOK

1½ POUNDS FILET MIGNON, CUBED

1 BUNCH WATERCRESS, HYDRO

1 MEDIUM RED ONION, SLICED

½ TEASPOON JAPANESE CHILI POWDER

serves 4

TO PREPARE THE VINAIGRETTE
In a bowl, combine the ground Thai chili,
lime juice, fish sauce, palm sugar, cilantro
and garlic. Set aside.

TO PREPARE THE BEEF
Add vegetable oil to wok, before searing
the filet mignon with sliced red onions
and Japanese chili powder. Shake back
and forth until beef is cooked to
desired doneness.

TO SERVE
Place the beef over a bed of watercress
and drizzle with the chili-lime vinaigrette.

NOTE: The name Shaking Beef comes
from the cooking technique. Substitute
red chili powder, if Japanese chili powder is unavailable. Fish sauce can seem
overpowering to some. Start with half the
amount and add to taste.

GREEN BEANS AND GUACAMOLE

1	POUND GREEN BEANS, TRIMMED
1	TEASPOON GARLIC, MINCED
1	TEASPOON FRESH GINGER, MINCED
1	TEASPOON FERMENTED BLACK BEANS
½	TEASPOON GREEN THAI CHILI, MINCED
1	OUNCE MUSHROOM SOY SAUCE
½	TEASPOON WHITE PEPPER
½	OUNCE SESAME OR VEGETABLE OIL

serves 4

Boil the green beans in a large pot of water until bright green. Drain and set aside to dry. Heat the sesame oil in a large skillet and sauté the garlic and ginger until soft. Add the green beans, fermented black beans, soy sauce and green Thai chili. Cook, stirring until the garlic and ginger brown and the beans become tender.

NOTE: Mushroom soy sauce can be found in Asian markets. Dark soy sauce may be substituted. If green Thai chilies are unavailable, substitute with a serrano or jalapeño.

HAVEN

GREEN BEANS AND GUACAMOLE

Chef Randy Evans' Haven restaurant has been well-received both locally and nationally since opening in 2009. The certified-green eatery, which was named a 'best new restaurant' by *Esquire* and *Southern Living* magazine, has flourished in its 5,200-square-foot, environmentally-friendly space. Raised-bed gardens are situated on-site, filled with herbs and vegetables used in Haven's kitchen. The outdoor area also makes room for composting and a rainwater cistern, which collects untreated water for the sustainable garden. Chef Evans' commitment to eco-conscious living is not only apparent in the restaurant's build out, but also throughout the modern Texas menu. The culinary line-up features a seasonally-changing selection of reimagined American cuisine like shrimp corn dogs with Tabasco-mash rémoulade and wild, head-on shrimp with shrimp boudin and andouille.

GREEN BEANS AND GUACAMOLE

WILD GULF SHRIMP CORN DOGS
with Tabasco mash rémoulade sauce

GULF SHRIMP CORN DOGS

12	EXTRA LARGE SHRIMP, PEELED AND DEVEINED
12	WOOD SKEWERS, 6 INCHES EACH
	KOSHER SALT AND BLACK PEPPER
1	CUP FLOUR, FOR DREDGING, SEASONED WITH SALT AND PEPPER
1½	CUPS CORNMEAL
¾	CUP FLOUR
½	PLUS ⅛ TEASPOONS BAKING SODA
¼	PLUS ⅛ TEASPOONS SALT
½	TABLESPOON TEXAS HONEY
¾	CUP BUTTERMILK
½	PLUS ⅛ CUP WATER
½	EGG

TO PREPARE THE CORN DOG

In a wide, shallow dish, combine the cornmeal, flour, baking soda, salt, honey, buttermilk, water and egg. Stir the batter until smooth. Skewer the shrimp lengthwise, starting at the tail end. Season the shrimp and dredge in seasoned flour. Roll the shrimp in the batter and fry in a 350°F fryer until golden brown.

TO PREPARE THE RÉMOULADE

Place all the ingredients, except for the oil, in a blender or food processor and mix at high speed until well blended. While processing, gradually add the oil in a slow, steady stream. Sauce will thicken to a creamy consistency. Adjust spice with the Tabasco mash. Store the sauce in a covered container in the refrigerator for up to 1 week.

TO SERVE

Serve with Tabasco mash dipping sauce and ice-cold Meyer lemonade.

TABASCO MASH RÉMOULADE

¼	CUP GREEN ONIONS, FINELY CHOPPED
2	TABLESPOONS CELERY, FINELY CHOPPED
2	TABLESPOONS PARSLEY, FINELY CHOPPED
2	TABLESPOONS KETCHUP
	PINCH TABASCO MASH OR 2 TABLESPOONS HORSERADISH AND A DASH OF TABASCO
2	TABLESPOONS CREOLE MUSTARD
1	TABLESPOON PREPARED YELLOW MUSTARD
1	TABLESPOON WHITE VINEGAR
2	TEASPOONS LEMON JUICE
¾	TEASPOON PAPRIKA
1	EGG
1	CLOVE GARLIC, MINCED
⅛	TEASPOON SALT
6	TABLESPOONS VEGETABLE OIL

serves 4

CRISPY PIG'S TROTTER FRITTERS

HAVEN

CRISPY TROTTERS

BRINED PIG'S FEET, SEE RECIPE

½ CUP CREOLE MUSTARD

½ HORSERADISH, FRESHLY GRATED

½ CUP STEEN'S CANE VINEGAR

2 TABLESPOONS GRANULATED ONION

1 TABLESPOON GRANULATED GARLIC

1 TEASPOON CAYENNE PEPPER

SALT AND PEPPER

1 EGG, LIGHTLY BEATEN

1 CUP ALL-PURPOSE FLOUR

2 CUPS BREAD CRUMBS

OIL, FOR FRYING

FRISÉE SALAD, SEE RECIPE

GIBSON COCKTAIL ONIONS, SEE RECIPE

AGED BALSAMIC VINEGAR, FOR DRIZZLING

FRESH, FLAT LEAF PARSLEY, FOR GARNISH

PIG'S FEET BRINE

2 TABLESPOONS OIL

½ LARGE ONION, CHOPPED

1 CELERY RIB, CHOPPED

1 CARROT, CHOPPED

1 JALAPEÑO PEPPER, CHOPPED

½ CUP APPLE, CHOPPED

1 LEMON, PEELED AND HALVED

2 CLOVES GARLIC

1 BAG ZATARAIN'S CRAB BOIL, 3 OUNCES

13 CUPS WATER, DIVIDED

½ CUP SALT

¼ CUP SUGAR

4 CUPS ICE

4 FRONT PIG'S FEET, INCLUDING THE SHANK AND FOOT

serves 4

TO PREPARE THE BRINED PIG'S FEET

Heat oil in a large saucepan over medium heat. Add the onions, carrots, celery, jalapeño, apple, lemon and garlic. Sweat for 3 minutes. Add the crab boil and 5 cups water. Bring to a simmer and continue to simmer for 30 minutes. Remove from heat. Place salt and sugar in a large container. Strain the spicy stock into the container. Stir until salt and sugar are dissolved. Add ice and remaining water, stir until ice is melted. Once cool, place the pork in the brine. Cover and marinate in the refrigerator overnight.

TO PREPARE THE TROTTERS

Remove the pork from the brine. In a large stockpot, cover the pork with pork stock or water and simmer, covered, for 3 to 4 hours or until it falls easily from the bone. Remove the meat, cartilage and a little of the skin from the meat. Transfer to a food processor. Combine with mustard, horseradish, vinegar, granulated onion, granulated garlic, cayenne and salt and pepper. Pulse in processor until combined, adding a little of the braising liquid to the mixture, if necessary. Refrigerate to chill. Once chilled, divide the meat mixture into 12 balls. Roll the balls in the flour, then in the lightly-beaten egg and then the bread crumbs. Shape the breaded meatballs into fritters or mini hockey pucks. Fry fritters in 350°F oil until golden. Remove onto a pan lined with paper towels.

TO PREPARE THE FRISÉE SALAD

In a bowl, add the garlic, shallots, basil, mustard and red wine vinegar. Stir to combine. Slowly whisk in the oil and then stir in the tomatoes and dash of Tabasco. Season with salt and pepper. Set aside. In a mixing bowl, combine ½ cup of the vinaigrette with frisée and toss until coated.

TO PREPARE THE COCKTAIL ONIONS

Combine salt and water in a non-reactive container and stir until salt is dissolved. Add the onions to brine and refrigerate overnight. Combine vinegar, sugar and pickling spice in a saucepot. Bring to a boil. Simmer for 15 minutes. Meanwhile, drain the onions from the brine and pack them snugly into properly sanitized jars. Ladle the hot vinegar over onions and seal, leaving a good ½-inch head space. Process the jars in a boiling water bath for 10 minutes. If preferred, store the onions under refrigeration to skip the canning procedure and store covered in the refrigerator. Allow to cure for two weeks before using.

TO SERVE

On a rectangular plate, spoon reserved vinaigrette along the center of the plate. Spread three tufts of salad on the plate and top with 3 fritters. Place a halved cocktail onion next to each fritter. Finally, drizzle with aged balsamic vinegar and garnish with 3 parsley leaves.

NOTE: To roast the tomatoes, cut 6 roma tomatoes in half, lengthwise, and place on a sheet pan. Drizzle with olive oil and sprinkle with salt and pepper. Broil on low heat until tomatoes lose more than half of their juice. Remove and cool. Pig's feet can be ordered from the butcher and sometimes comes frozen.

FRISÉE SALAD

2 HEADS FRISÉE LETTUCE, CLEANED AND STEMS REMOVED

1 TEASPOON GARLIC, MINCED

1 TABLESPOON SHALLOTS, MINCED

1½ TABLESPOONS BASIL, CHOPPED

3 TABLESPOONS DIJON MUSTARD

2 TABLESPOONS RED WINE VINEGAR

1 CUP OLIVE OIL

½ CUP ROASTED ROMA TOMATOES, DICED, SEE NOTE

DASH TABASCO SAUCE

SALT AND PEPPER

GIBSON COCKTAIL ONIONS

¼ CUP COARSE SEA SALT

4 CUPS WATER

1 PINT TINY PEARL ONIONS, PEELED

2 CUPS CHAMPAGNE VINEGAR

3 TABLESPOONS SUGAR

1 TABLESPOON PICKLING SPICE

HUGO'S

It's been more than 25 years since Mexico City-born Chef Hugo Ortega put down roots in Houston. In the time since, he's worked his way through the restaurant ranks as line cook at Prego, Executive Chef at Backstreet Cafe and now as the culinary brainchild behind his Montrose-set namesake. There, he serves up authentic, regional Mexican cuisine that's gained national attention, including a spot on *Bon Appetit* magazine's "Top Table" list. Settle into the inviting, hacienda-style space with its Saltillo-tile floors, wood accents, hand-tooled leather chairs and stamped tin ceiling. Expect a menu filled with modernized Mexico City classics: Achiote-marinated pork ribs, lobster tacos and *chapulines*—pan-sautéed grasshoppers served with guacamole, tortillas and chipotle-tamatillo salsa. Keep an eye out for Chef Ortega's seasonal squash blossom menu, offered during the summer

HUGO'S

1 POUND FRESH SNAPPER, HALIBUT OR OTHER MEATY FISH, CUT INTO ¼-INCH THICK BY ½-INCH LONG STRIPS

1½ CUPS LIME JUICE

1 MEDIUM WHITE ONION, CHOPPED INTO ½-INCH PIECES

1 POUND RIPE PLUM TOMATOES, CHOPPED INTO ½-INCH PIECES

2-3 SERRANO PEPPERS OR JALAPEÑOS, FINELY CHOPPED

⅓ CUP CILANTRO, CHOPPED

⅓ CUP MANZANILLA OLIVES

1-2 TABLESPOONS OLIVE OIL

SALT

3 TABLESPOONS FRESH ORANGE JUICE

1 LARGE OR 2 SMALL RIPE AVOCADOS, PEELED, SEEDED AND THINLY SLICED

TOSTADA CHIPS, FOR SERVING

makes 5 cups

In a large bowl, combine the fish, lime juice and onion. The juice should cover the fish. Marinate for three hours in the refrigerator. Drain juices and combine with remaining ingredients. Garnish with avocado slices and cilantro sprigs and serve with tostadas.

GREEN BEANS AND GUACAMOLE

GUACAMOLE,
HUGO'S

6	TOMATILLOS, QUARTERED
½	BUNCH FRESH CILANTRO
¼	RED ONION, DICED
2	SERRANO PEPPERS
4	AVOCADOS, PEELED, SEEDED AND MASHED
2	ROMA TOMATOES, DICED
½	TEASPOON OLIVE OIL
1	LIME, JUICED
	SALT AND PEPPER

serves 4

Juice the tomatillos, cilantro, onion and serrano peppers, see note below. Save the pulp and discard the juice. In a medium bowl, mix together the pulp, avocado, tomatoes, olive oil and lime juice. Stir well to incorporate. Season to taste with salt and pepper.

NOTE: Without a juicer, purée tomatillos, cilantro, onion and serrano peppers in a blender. Pass through a fine sieve to separate pulp from juice. Use a wooden spoon or spatula to press as much juice through the sieve as possible.

IBIZA

Midtown's Ibiza restaurant never stops buzzing with excitement. Maybe it's the well-priced wine list, popular patio, tableside cocktail cart or Chef Charles Clark's Mediterranean-inspired menu—whatever the reason, locals keep coming back night-after-night. Awash in cool blues, Ibiza's interior features an open kitchen, a French-door-lined exterior and a 25-foot wall-of-wine. The hotspot—which Chef Clark co-owns with restaurant partner Grant Cooper—melds culinary techniques from France, Italy and Spain, serving a mix of small plates and main courses. The Basque green pepper and crab bisque, the braised lamb shank and grilled-shrimp with goat cheese polenta are all delicious. Join other style-savvy patrons for post-dinner drinks at Ibiza's Lounge Next Door.

TEXAS PEACHES
with fresh mint, toasted spanish almonds and Frangelico

2 POUNDS FRESH TEXAS PEACHES

½ CUP FRESH MINT LEAVES

2 TABLESPOONS SPANISH ALMONDS, SLICED

½ CUP FRANGELICO

2 PINTS BLUE BELL VANILLA ICE CREAM

serves 6

Preheat oven to 350°F.

Wash, peel and seed peaches, then slice into thin pieces and set aside. Wash mint and gently slice, do not chop, into thin strips and set aside. Spread almonds onto a cookie sheet and toast in the oven for about 5 to 7 minutes. Remove almonds from oven and set aside. In a large bowl, combine the peaches, mint, almonds and Frangelico. Refrigerate for 4 hours until well chilled. Place a scoop of vanilla ice cream into a margarita glass or other serving dish, top evenly with peach mixture.

PAN-SEARED SCALLOPS
with summer radish succotash

6	LARGE SCALLOPS
5	OUNCES SHITAKE MUSHROOMS, SHAVED PAPER-THIN
5	OUNCES FRENCH GREEN BEANS, BLANCHED UNTIL SWEET, ABOUT 4 MINUTES
5	OUNCES RAW RED RADISH, SHAVED PAPER-THIN USING A MANDOLINE
3	OUNCES ENGLISH PEAS
5	OUNCES FRESH CORN KERNELS, STEAMED
1	OUNCE BABY ARUGULA
2	OUNCES SHALLOTS, MINCED
1	TABLESPOON PARMESAN CHEESE, GRATED
2	TABLESPOONS EXTRA VIRGIN OLIVE OIL
1	TEASPOON UNSALTED BUTTER
2	WHOLE LEMONS
	SEA SALT
	SALT AND PEPPER

serves 6 (small plates)

Season scallops with salt and pepper. Set aside. Heat a large sauté pan for about 10 minutes or until hot. Add olive oil to pan, then place seasoned scallops in pan and sear until golden brown on both sides, about 6 minutes. Set aside and keep warm. Using the same pan, add butter and shallots and sauté until shallots are brown, about 5 minutes. Add mushrooms, green beans, radish, peas, corn and arugula and fold together over heat for 1 minute. Add Parmesan cheese. Distribute mixture evenly among 6, small appetizer plates. Add a seared scallop on top of each mixture and garnish with a squeeze of fresh lemon and sea salt.

INDIKA

GREEN BEANS AND GUACAMOLE

Inspired by the regional cuisines of India, Chef/Owner Anita Jaisinghani transforms traditional ingredients into innovative dishes at Indika. Authentic in both fire and flavor, her cuisine is progressive, moving the boundaries of taste with dishes like baby lamb chops with a mint masala, pickled eggplant and saffron potatoes. Creativity abounds in the black lentil chilla with a spicy market vegetable masala, tomato mustard curry and coconut chutney. Indika is lauded for crab samosas, lamb shanks and corn and mint chaat, and those in-the-know never pass on the bread pudding. One of Chef Jaisinghani's personal favorites? The beet soup.

DAL MAKHNI
INDIKA

2 CUPS YELLOW MOONG LENTILS

4 CUPS WATER

1 TEASPOON TURMERIC

2 SERRANO PEPPERS, MINCED

2 TEASPOONS SALT

3 TABLESPOONS CLARIFIED BUTTER

1 TABLESPOON CUMIN SEED

3 LARGE GARLIC CLOVES, SLICED

2 MEDIUM ROMA TOMATOES, DICED

2 TABLESPOONS CILANTRO, CHOPPED

1 LEMON, JUICED

serves 8

Soak the lentils in warm water for 1 to 2 hours. Drain and rinse. Put the lentils in a deep stockpot and add the water, turmeric, serrano peppers and salt. Bring to a boil, then lower heat and simmer covered for 20 to 30 minutes or until tender. Stir gently, so as not to break up the lentils. In a shallow saucepan, heat the clarified butter over medium-high heat until not quite smoking. Add the cumin seed and allow it to pop. Then add the garlic slices and cook for a few seconds. Stir in the tomatoes, then add the mixture to the lentils. Just before serving, add the lemon juice. Garnish with the chopped cilantro.

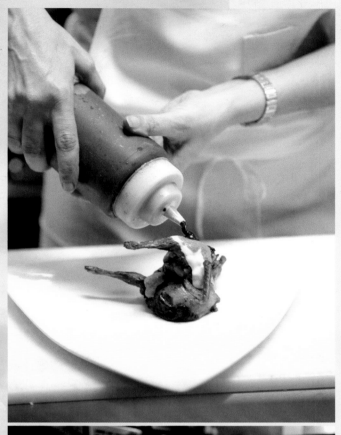

QUAIL

4	SEMI-BONELESS QUAIL
3	TABLESPOONS OLIVE OIL
2	TABLESPOONS MANGO CHUTNEY
2	TEASPOONS SALT
2	TEASPOONS PEPPER

STUFFING

1	MEDIUM ONION, SLICED AND FRIED IN A LITTLE OIL UNTIL BROWNED
¾	CUP PINE NUTS, TOASTED
1	TABLESPOON DRIED FENUGREEK LEAVES
1	TABLESPOON KASHMIRI CHILI POWDER, SEE NOTE
2	CLOVES GARLIC, MINCED
1	TEASPOON GARAM MASALA
1	TEASPOON SALT

serves 2

Preheat oven to 350°F.

TO PREPARE THE PINE-NUT STUFFING
Combine the olive oil, chutney, salt and pepper in a small bowl. Rub the quail with the mixture and marinate for up to 2 hours. Grind half of the pine nuts in a coffee grinder to a smooth consistency. Place in a small bowl and stir in the onion, remaining pine nuts, fenugreek, chili powder, garlic, garam masala and salt.

TO PREPARE THE QUAIL
Stuff the quail with the pine nut stuffing and tie with butcher's twine. Grill the quail on a hot grill for 3 to 4 minutes, per side. Finish cooking in a 350°F oven for another 10 to 12 minutes. Let the quail rest for a few minutes after removing from the oven. Slice each quail in half and serve.

NOTE: Ground New Mexican ancho or other "pure" chili powders may be substituted. Do not use the prepared chili powder available in supermarkets, which usually includes garlic, cumin, oregano and other seasonings.

GREEN BEANS AND GUACAMOLE

KIRAN'S

Just west of Highland Village, Chef Kiran Verma can be found as much in the kitchen as she can out front, greeting and receiving diners at her namesake restaurant. Serving regal food in the Mughlai-style of Northern India, Chef Kiran fuses her Indian dishes with French presentation techniques, creating a fine dining experience that stands out in the city. House specialties include sea bass, lobster, lamb, game, exotic vegetables and handmade chutneys. Try the jumbo lump crab salad, the soup flight and the trio of crème brûlée—saffron, cardamom and pistachio. The extensive wine collection, which *Wine Spectator* recognizes each year with an Award of Excellence, is carefully chosen to complement Kiran's menu.

GREEN BEANS AND GUACAMOLE

LAMB KEEMA
KIRAN'S

LAMB

6	OUNCES COOKING OIL
12	OUNCES ONIONS, CHOPPED
6	OUNCES GINGER AND GARLIC PASTE
1	OUNCE TURMERIC POWDER
1	OUNCE CAYENNE PEPPER OR CHILI POWDER
2	POUNDS GROUND LAMB LEG, ALL FAT TRIMMED
4	TOMATOES, PURÉED
4	OUNCES PLAIN YOGURT
2	OUNCES GARAM MASALA, SEE RECIPE AND NOTE
2	TABLESPOONS GREEN CHILIES, MINCED
1	TABLESPOON KOSHER SALT
1	BUNCH FRESH CILANTRO, FINELY CHOPPED
6	SERVINGS COOKED RICE OR PASTA

GARAM MASALA

1	OUNCE CUMIN, WHOLE
1	OUNCE CORIANDER, WHOLE
½	OUNCE BLACK CARDAMOM, WHOLE
½	OUNCE GREEN CARDAMOM, WHOLE
½	OUNCE CLOVES, WHOLE
½	OUNCE BLACK PEPPERCORN, WHOLE
½	OUNCE CINNAMON, WHOLE
½	OUNCE MACE, WHOLE

GARNISH

2	OUNCES BUTTER
1	OUNCE BABY GREEN PEAS
4	CHERRY TOMATOES
6	GINGER SLIVERS
½	MEDIUM RED ONION

serves 6

TO PREPARE GARAM MASALA
Combine all ingredients in coffee grinder until finely ground. Makes 5 ounces more than is needed in recipe. Store in the freezer. Stays good for one year.

TO PREPARE THE LAMB
Heat oil in large, heavy-bottom pot. Add onions and cook until light brown. Add ginger and garlic paste, cook for 2 minutes. Add turmeric powder and cayenne pepper or chili powder. Add ground lamb. Cook for 5 minutes or until lamb browns and appears cooked. Add salt to taste. Add tomatoes and yogurt. Cook for 5 minutes. Add 1 tablespoon garam masala and the minced chilies. Cook for 5 minutes. Remove from heat and stir in cilantro.

TO PREPARE GARNISH
Combine all ingredients and sauté.

TO SERVE LAMB KEEMA
Spoon prepared rice or pasta onto plates. Top with lamb mixture and prepared garnish.

NOTE: Prepared garam masala can be found in Indian food markets and gourmet grocery stores and is a suitable alternative to the freshly-ground recipe included here.

TO PREPARE PICKLING SPICES
Combine all ingredients in a small bowl.

TO PREPARE THE OKRA
In a medium skillet, heat cooking oil over high heat until it has reached a smoking point. Turn down to medium heat and add the pickling spices. Add the onions and sauté until translucent. Add the ginger and garlic and lightly sauté. Add the okra, salt to taste, mango powder, fresh coconut and green chilies. Stir to combine. Add the chopped tomatoes and the lemon juice. Sauté until the okra is tender. Garnish with coconut. Serve with bread or naan.

NOTE: Okra is at its peak in the summer. Select small and tender pods. To save time, begin by flash frying the okra in 2 ounces of clean vegetable oil at 375°F and then proceed with recipe. Pickling spices and other less common spices can be found in specialty markets or online.

2	POUNDS FRESH OKRA, SMALL AND TENDER, CHOPPED INTO THIN, CIRCULAR DISCS
4	OUNCES VEGETABLE OIL OR 2 OUNCES, IF YOU FLASH FRY OKRA, SEE NOTE
	PICKLING SPICES, SEE RECIPE BELOW
1	CUP RED ONION, CHOPPED
1	OUNCE GINGER, MINCED
2	OUNCES GARLIC, MINCED
1	TABLESPOON KOSHER SALT
1	TABLESPOON MANGO POWDER
1	TABLESPOON FRESHLY-GRATED COCONUT, FOR COOKING
4	GREEN CHILIES, SEEDED AND MINCED
2	MEDIUM, FIRM ROMA TOMATOES, CUT INTO 8 CUBES
1	LEMON, JUICED
½	TEASPOON FRESHLY-GRATED COCONUT, FOR GARNISH
	BREAD OF NAAN, FOR SERVING

PICKLING SPICES

½	TEASPOON MUSTARD SEEDS
½	TEASPOON METHI (FENUGREEK) SEEDS
½	TEASPOON KALONJI (ONION) SEEDS
½	TEASPOON FENNEL SEEDS
½	TEASPOON CORIANDER SEEDS
6	DRIED, WHOLE RED CHILIES

serves 6

GREEN BEANS AND GUACAMOLE

LE MISTRAL

Repeatedly voted as one of Houston's top French restaurants, Le Mistral puts a Provençal spin on regional Gallic cuisine. Co-owner/Chef David Denis grew up in the Provence region of France, working at his mother and grandmother's restaurants, before attending culinary school at Ecole du Beusset, where he finished first in his class. He eventually moved to Houston and, along with his architect/brother Sylvain, opened Le Mistral. There, Chef David's experience shines in the Gruyère-topped onion soup, osso bucco and the seared sea scallops with leeks julienne and carbonara-smoked salmon. After dinner, venture next door to Foody's Gourmet and Bakery—the brothers' specialty food store and home to the restaurant's wine and cooking classes.

TOMATO TARTAR & TOMATO BASIL SORBET
with Parmesan crisp

LE MISTRAL

TOMATO BASIL SORBET

½ LITER TOMATO JUICE

3 OUNCES BASIL, THINLY SLICED

SALT AND PEPPER

PARMESAN CRISP

2 CUPS PARMESAN CHEESE, SHREDDED

TOMATO TARTAR

2 HEIRLOOM TOMATOES

2 YELLOW TOMATOES

2 CUPS RED GRAPE TOMATOES

1 GREEN TOMATO

1 TABLESPOON SHALLOT, CHOPPED FINE

1 TABLESPOON ITALIAN PARSLEY, CHOPPED FINE

1 TABLESPOON FRENCH PICKLES, CHOPPED, ALSO KNOWN AS CORNICHONS

2 TABLESPOONS EXTRA VIRGIN OLIVE OIL

SALT AND PEPPER

BASIL WATER

½ CUP EXTRA VIRGIN OLIVE OIL

10 OUNCES BASIL, FRESH

1 CUP CHICKEN STOCK

SALT AND PEPPER

serves 4

Preheat oven to 375°F.

TO PREPARE THE SORBET
Combine all ingredients and place in an ice cream maker. Reserve the ice cream for later.

TO PREPARE THE PARMESAN CRISP
Place Parmesan on the sheet pan and bake until it becomes golden. Remove from oven and set aside.

TO PREPARE THE TOMATO TARTAR
Bring a pot of water to a boil. Cut a shallow cross or X on the end of each tomato. Drop them into the boiling water for a few seconds and immediately remove and plunge them into ice water. Drain and remove the skins. Cube the tomatoes and place them in a bowl. Add the remaining ingredients to the tomatoes and place in the refrigerator to chill.

TO PREPARE THE BASIL WATER
Bring the chicken stock to a boil in a pan. Add the basil for 20 seconds and then remove and chill in cold water. Let the chicken stock cool. Once cool, put all of the ingredients into a blender and blend until smooth.

TO SERVE
Pour the basil water into the bottom of each plate. Using a ring mold, shape the tomato tartar. Remove the mold. Place the Parmesan crisp on top of the tomato tartar. Make a canella of the tomato sorbet and place on top of the crisp.

NOTE:
Recipe is equally as satisfying without the sorbet.

GREEN BEANS AND GUACAMOLE

ROASTED CHILEAN SEA BASS
on a smoked tomato broth

Preheat oven to 375°F.

TO PREPARE THE TOMATO BROTH
Soak the wood chips in the water. Cut the tomatoes into four pieces. Remove the wood chips from water, towel dry them and place them in a metal bowl. Put the tomatoes onto a sheet pan with tall sides. Place the bowl of wood chips onto the same pan. Light the wood chips. Once they begin to smoke, cover the entire sheet pan—with the tomatoes and wood chip bowl—with plastic film for 15 minutes until there is a light smoke. Let the tomatoes rest. Place the tomatoes into a blender and add the olive oil, chicken stock, clam juice and blend until smooth. Pass the liquid through a sieve. Place the bay leaf in the liquid and set aside.

TO PREPARE THE BALSAMIC GLAZE
Place all of the ingredients in a pot over medium heat and let reduce for 40 minutes until it becomes a thick syrup.

TO PREPARE THE BEET GARNISH
Thinly slice one beet and shred the remaining beets to make long strings. Heat the oil. Separately, deep-fry the beets for about 2 minutes. Remove the beets and place on a paper towel to drain. Sprinkle with sea salt.

TO PREPARE THE SEA BASS
Melt the butter in a sauté pan. Salt and pepper the bass. Slowly sear the fish on each side. Place in a preheated oven for 8 minutes.

TO SERVE
Warm up the tomato broth and place in a large bowl or on a plate. Place the fish in the middle. Surround the fish with the balsamic glaze. Top the fish with the beet chip, then top the chip with the beet string. Place 2 chive sprigs on top of the beet.

NOTE: Liquid smoke can be used, in place of the wood chips, for the tomato broth.

SMOKED TOMATO BROTH

10	TOMATOES
1	CUP EXTRA VIRGIN OLIVE OIL
1½	CUPS CHICKEN STOCK
1	CUP CLAM JUICE
1	BAY LEAF
	WOOD CHIPS
1	CUP WATER

BALSAMIC GLAZE

1	CUP BALSAMIC VINEGAR
1	CUP VEAL STOCK
1	CUP WATER

BEET GARNISH

2	LARGE RED BEETS
4	CUPS FRYING OIL
8	SPRIGS CHIVES
	SEA SALT

CHILEAN SEA BASS

4	SEA BASS FILLETS, 6 OUNCES EACH
2	TABLESPOONS BUTTER
	SALT AND PEPPER

serves 4

GREEN BEANS AND GUACAMOLE

MARK'S

Some might say that dining at Mark's is a religious experience—after all, the romantic restaurant *is* set inside Montrose's nearly 100-year-old St. Matthews Church. Built in the 1920s—and renovated by chef and owner Mark Cox in 1997—the cozy space is striking with hand-painted deco walls, golden accents and stained glass windows. Beneath the vaulted sanctuary, Chef Cox takes diners on an epicurean adventure, filled with reimagined American fare. His progressive array of dishes are highlighted on multiple menus, which change throughout the day. Some of Mark's historic, stand-out creations include the Kobe beef osso buco, Copper River salmon, fresh Alaskan king crab legs and spiny lobster tails. Finish in sin with the warm chocolate cake.

GREEN BEANS AND GUACAMOLE

THAI SHRIMP AND CRAB CAKE

2 CLOVES GARLIC
8 OUNCES SEA BASS
¼ POUND RAW SHRIMP
5 TABLESPOONS LIME JUICE
1 EGG WHITE
2 TEASPOONS GINGER, MINCED
1 TABLESPOON FISH SAUCE
1 TABLESPOON CORNSTARCH
1 TEASPOON SAMBAL CHILI SAUCE
1 TEASPOON SUGAR
8 OUNCES CRABMEAT, ½ JUMBO LUMP, ½ LUMP
8 OUNCES SHRIMP, COOKED, CUT INTO ½-INCH PIECES, BOILED AND CHILLED
¼ CUP CILANTRO, CHOPPED
¼ CUP RED BELL PEPPER, FINELY DICED
KOSHER SALT AND WHITE PEPPER
1½ TABLESPOONS OLIVE OIL

MUSHROOM BROTH

¼ CUP GRAPESEED OIL
3 POUNDS BUTTON MUSHROOMS, SLICED
1 ONION, PEELED AND COARSELY CHOPPED
3 CLOVES GARLIC, COARSELY CHOPPED
¾ CUP WHITE WINE
2 TABLESPOONS SHERRY VINEGAR
1 QUART WATER
2 SPRIGS THYME
5 BLACK PEPPERCORNS
10 SPRIGS ITALIAN PARSLEY
1 BAY LEAF
2 TABLESPOONS SHOA XING RICE WATER
1 TABLESPOON MIRIN
2 TABLESPOONS FISH SAUCE

serves 6

Marinate the Sea Bass for 12 hours with miso mirin marinade. Preheat oven to 350°F.

TO PREPARE THE MISO MIRIN MARINADE
Applicable to either version. Combine sugar and liquids in a saucepan, heat just until the sugar dissolves. Remove from heat and whisk in the miso. Allow to cool to room temperature, then coat fish completely and put in a roasting pan lined with paper towels. Cover and refrigerate for at least 12 hours.

TO PREPARE THE THAI SHRIMP AND CRAB CAKE
Finely grind garlic in a blender. Add next 9 ingredients—from 8 ounces sea bass to 1 teaspoon sugar—and grind into an even paste. In a bowl, combine the crabmeat, shrimp, cilantro and red bell pepper. Gently fold in the paste, being careful not to break up the jumbo lump crabmeat. Season to taste with kosher salt and white pepper. Mold into 3, ½-ounce cakes using a ring mold. Heat olive oil in a non-stick pan. Sear the shrimp and crab cake on both sides, about 2 to 3 minutes per side, until cooked through. Set aside.

TO PREPARE THE MUSHROOM BROTH
Sauté mushrooms in oil until golden brown. Add onions and garlic and cook until tender. Add the wine and vinegar and bring to a simmer, cooking 2 minutes. Add water, thyme, peppercorns, parsley and bay leaf. Bring to a boil and then simmer until reduced by ⅔. Do not continue to boil. Remove from heat and pass through a sieve, making sure to press out as much liquid as possible. Finish by adding the Shoa Xing, mirin and fish sauce. Set aside and keep warm.

TO PREPARE THE FRIED SHALLOTS
Using a mandoline, slice shallots as thinly as possible. Pour oil into a small, heavy pot to a depth of 1 inch and heat over medium-high heat until a deep-fry thermometer registers 325°F. Working in batches of no more than a handful, add shallots to oil and fry, stirring, until light golden brown. Remove shallots from oil, with a slotted spoon, and spread evenly on a paper towel-lined plate to drain. Shallots will continue to cook and will further crisp. Set aside to cool. Makes approximately 2 cups and can be stored in an airtight container, lined with paper towels, for up to 3 days.

TO PREPARE THE SEA BASS
Remove the fish from the marinade and discard the marinade. Pat the fish dry. Heat a sauté pan over medium heat. Add the olive oil and sauté 2 Sea Bass fillets at a time until lightly golden brown. Transfer Sea Bass to a baking pan and bake for 8 to 10 minutes or until cooked through.

TO SERVE
In a bowl or deep plate, pour some broth. Place the shrimp and crab cake in the center. Place the Sea Bass on top. Garnish with fried shallots.

CHILEAN SEA BASS

8 CHILEAN SEA BASS FILLETS, 6-8½ OUNCES EACH
1½ TABLESPOONS OLIVE OIL
SALT AND PEPPER

FRIED SHALLOTS

6 SHALLOTS
PEANUT OIL

MISO MIRIN MARINADE

TWO VERSIONS OF MISO, USE EITHER BASED ON PREFERENCE

WHITE MISO

1 CUP WHITE MISO PASTE
¾ CUP MIRIN
¾ CUP SAKE
3 TABLESPOONS BROWN SUGAR

RED MISO

½ CUP RED MISO PASTE
½ CUP MIRIN
¼ CUP SAKE
3 TABLESPOONS BROWN SUGAR

Preheat oven to 350°F.

TO PREPARE THE GARNISH
Using a non-stick pan over medium heat, melt the butter until golden. Add the 4 ounces of corn kernels and lightly season with salt and pepper. Place in the oven and roast for 7 to 10 minutes, stirring as needed. Roast to a rich golden brown. Remove and set aside.

TO PREPARE THE CORN CHOWDER
In a medium sauce pan, sauté the bacon over medium heat until crispy and golden brown. Remove the bacon and place on paper towels to drain. In the pan with the bacon drippings, add the garlic, onions and celery, stirring occasionally for 5 minutes. Add the potatoes and chicken stock. Bring to a boil and simmer 5 minutes. Add the corn and continue to simmer for 5 more minutes. Add the heavy cream, bring to a boil, then simmer 7 minutes. Remove from the heat and add the lime juice, thyme and crispy bacon. Season with salt and pepper as needed.

TO SERVE
Ladle into bowls. Garnish with chives and roasted corn.

GARNISH

4	OUNCES WHOLE CORN KERNELS
½	TABLESPOON UNSALTED BUTTER

CORN CHOWDER

1	CUP APPLE-SMOKED BACON, DICED MEDIUM
1	TABLESPOON GARLIC, FINELY CHOPPED
1	CUP YELLOW ONION, DICED MEDIUM
1	CUP CELERY, DICED MEDIUM
1	CUP RED POTATOES WITH SKIN, DICED MEDIUM
8	OUNCES FRESH CORN KERNELS, DICED BY HAND OR PULSED IN PROCESSOR
3	CUPS CHICKEN STOCK
2	CUPS HEAVY CREAM
¼	TO ½ TEASPOON SALT
¼	TEASPOON GROUND WHITE PEPPER
1	TABLESPOON LIME JUICE
1	TABLESPOON FRESH THYME
2	TABLESPOONS CHIVES, THINLY SLICED

serves 4

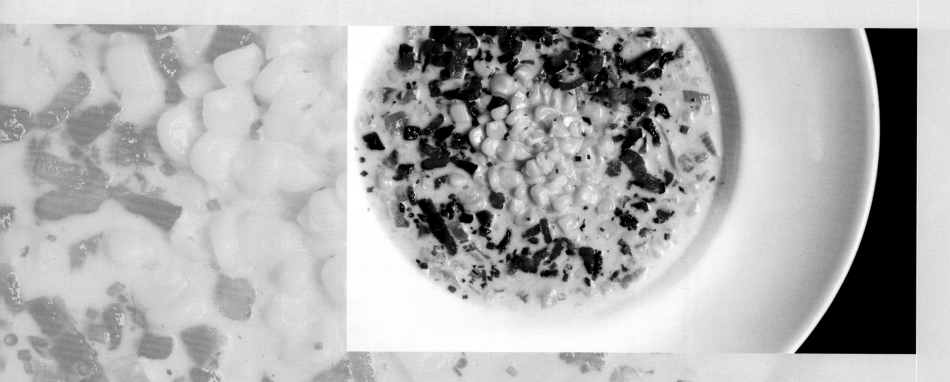

GREEN BEANS AND GUACAMOLE

MASRAFF'S

GREEN BEANS AND GUACAMOLE

It's been more than a decade since father-son team Tony and Russell Masraff teamed up to launch the family's contemporary-American concept. The duo's namesake restaurant, which was originally located on South Post Oak Lane, moved to its renovated Post Oak digs in spring 2010. Set in the heart of the Galleria area, the light-filled and modern space features floor-to-ceiling windows, etched-metal artwork, a 10-foot-high elevated fireplace and shimmering light fixtures designed by Tony and Russell. Masraff's front-facing patio is a popular perch with guests, boasting a covered awning and 60-foot-long water feature that helps mask the bustle of the Boulevard. The popular wild-mushroom ravioli and garlic-seared calamari both impress on the variety-filled menu, as do the daily-changing risottos and the caramelized diver scallops. Don't forget to say hello to the Masraff's, who are often on hand to greet customers.

GREEN BEANS AND GUACAMOLE

151

POACHED BLUE SHRIMP AND CRAB NAPOLEON

NAPOLEON

5 JUMBO BLUE SHRIMP, PER PERSON, EACH POACHED AND SLICED IN HALF

5 OUNCES COLOSSAL CRABMEAT, SEE NOTE

½ CUP MANGO, DICED SMALL

½ CUP AVOCADO, DICED SMALL

¼ CUP RED ONION, DICED SMALL

¼ CUP CILANTRO, CLEANED AND CHOPPED

¼ CUP BASIL, CHOPPED

½ CUP AVOCADO MOUSSE, SEE RECIPE

8 WONTON CHIPS, EACH CUT INTO 3-INCH DIAMETER ROUNDS, FRIED

BLACK SESAME SEEDS, FOR GARNISH

MICROGREENS, FOR GARNISH

AVOCADO MOUSSE

1 AVOCADO, DICED

2 TABLESPOONS LEMON JUICE

2 TABLESPOONS ORANGE JUICE

3 OUNCES SEASONED RICE WINE VINEGAR

2 TEASPOONS KOSHER SALT

4 OUNCES GRAPESEED OIL

1 TEASPOON RAYU PURE SESAME OIL

serves 4

TO PREPARE THE AVOCADO MOUSSE

Place the first 5 ingredients—from avocado to kosher salt—into a blender and purée until smooth. Slowly add the grapeseed oil and then slowly add the sesame oil. Place in a squeeze bottle and refrigerate.

TO PREPARE THE NAPOLEON

In a medium bowl, add the shrimp, crab, mango, avocado, red onion, cilantro, basil and avocado mousse. Gently fold the ingredients together. Place a 1-ounce dollop in the center of 4 separate plates. Place a wonton chip on top of each. Repeat with an additional dollop of seafood mixture and an additional wonton. Drizzle mousse on plate and garnish with sesame seeds and micro greens.

NOTE: Colossal crab is mega jumbo lump, the largest whole, unbroken pieces from blue crab. It is bigger than jumbo lump. Pita chips can be substituted, if wontons aren't available.

BOSC PEAR CRÈME BRÛLÉE
in berry soup

Preheat oven to 350°F.

TO PREPARE THE SUGAR-ROASTED PEARS
Place pears, sugar and soft butter in medium-size bowl. Rub the butter on the pears evenly so that the sugar coats the pears. Place the pears on a non-stick sheet tray and roast at 350°F for 25 minutes. Remove from oven. Set aside to cool.

TO PREPARE THE BERRY SOUP
Place all ingredients, except sugar, in a small saucepan. Bring to a boil and simmer 5 minutes. Turn off fire, then fold in sugar, until dissolved, and let cool.

TO PREPARE THE CRÈME BRÛLÉE
Preheat the oven to 325°F. Place the cream, vanilla bean and its pulp into a medium saucepan, set over medium-high heat, and bring to a boil. Remove from heat, stir in a ½-cup of sugar, cover and allow to sit for 15 minutes. Remove the vanilla bean and reserve for another use. In a medium bowl, whisk together a ½-cup sugar and the egg yolks, until well-blended and just starting to lighten in color. Add the cream a little at a time, stirring continually. Pour the liquid into a glass baking dish. Place the baking dish into a large cake pan or roasting pan. Pour enough hot water into the pan to come half-way up. Bake just until the crème brûlée is set, but still trembling in the center—approximately 40 to 45 minutes. Remove the half-cake pan from the roasting pan and refrigerate for at least 2 hours and up to 3 days.

TO PREPARE THE CRÈME BRÛLÉE IN BERRY SOUP
Split pear down the center, length-wise. Scoop out the center with a medium-size ice cream scoop. Place berry soup in bowl, then scoop out 1 round scoop of the crème mix and place it inside the pear. Sprinkle sugar on top of the crème, then proceed to burn the top with a torch, until crispy. Place stuffed pear in the center of the bowl and serve.

4	BOSC PEARS, SUGAR-ROASTED
2	CUPS WHOLE-BERRY SOUP
16	OUNCES COOKED CRÈME BRÛLÉE
2	TABLESPOONS SUGAR

SUGAR-ROASTED PEARS

4	BOSC PEARS, SPLIT IN HALF
4	OUNCES BUTTER, SOFTENED
¼	CUP SUGAR

BERRY SOUP

2	CUPS MIXED, FROZEN BERRIES
2	TABLESPOONS LEMON JUICE
2	TABLESPOONS ORANGE JUICE
½	CUP WATER
1	CUP SUGAR

CRÈME BRÛLÉE

1	QUART HEAVY CREAM
1	VANILLA BEAN, SPLIT AND SCRAPED
1	CUP VANILLA SUGAR, DIVIDED
6	LARGE EGG YOLKS
2	QUARTS HOT WATER

serves 8

MAX'S WINE DIVE

"Fried chicken and Champagne? Why the hell not?!" Comfort food goes gourmet at Washington Avenue's Max's Wine Dive. The cheeky wine bar—created and owned by The Tasting Room folks—doesn't take itself too seriously. From the fresh-faced clientele to the fun, personality-filled menu touting Texas "Haute" dogs and shrimp and grits, Max's is all about delivering a good time. Of course, the dive is serious about its wine, too, with an extensive line-up that is always changing and well priced. See something you like? The restaurant will open any bottle for guests willing to purchase at least two glasses. Want to impress that special someone? Make a reservation for Max's Urban Picnic—a custom-created getaway, set inside the bustling restaurant. The experience comes complete with basket, iconic checked tablecloth, cold fried chicken and more.

TO PREPARE THE TRUFFLE MAYO

Place the mayo in a small bowl and stir in the truffle cream until evenly dispersed. Place in refrigerator.

TO PREPARE THE CHILI BACON

In a hot skillet, place a small amount of olive oil and add the onions. Allow the onions to sweat until they start to caramelize. Add the tomatoes and jalapeño. Cook for 1 minute. Add the habanero salsa, bacon and lime juice. Reduce to a medium consistency. Remove from heat and add cilantro. Set aside.

TO PREPARE THE SANDWICH

Lightly butter the bread and place in heated skillet. Toast both sides. Remove and set aside. Place the eggs in skillet making sure not to break the yolk. Once the white of the eggs have set, turn them over. Place the cheese on top of the eggs, then add the chili bacon. Cook 30 more seconds. Remove from heat. Liberally spread the truffle mayo on the bread. Place the egg, cheese and bacon combination on top. Add the tomato slices and season with salt and pepper. Place the Bibb lettuce on top and add the top piece of bread.

NOTE: Pugliese is a rustic Italian bread and can be substituted, if difficult to find, with a sourdough or ciabatta. See Appendix for Slow Dough's ciabatta recipe. Truffle cream can be found in specialty markets and online.

FRIED EGG SANDWICH

3	EGGS
2	SLICES OF PUGLIESE BREAD, SEE NOTE
¼	CUP GRUYÈRE CHEESE
2	SLICES TOMATO
1	LEAF OF HYDROPONIC BIBB LETTUCE

TRUFFLE MAYO

¼	CUP MAYONNAISE
½	TEASPOON TRUFFLE CREAM

CHILI BACON

1	JALAPEÑO, MINCED
¼	ONION, DICED SMALL
½	TOMATO, DICED SMALL
½	CUP HABANERO SALSA
4	STRIPS BACON, COOKED
1	LIME, JUICED
3	SPRIGS CILANTRO, LEAVES ONLY
	SALT AND PEPPER
	EXTRA VIRGIN OLIVE OIL

serves 1

GREEN BEANS AND GUACAMOLE

HOUSE-PICKLED JALAPEÑOS

- 1¼ POUNDS JALAPEÑOS
- ¼ POUND CARROTS
- ¼ POUND YELLOW ONIONS
- 1 CUP WATER
- ½ TEASPOON OREGANO
- 1¼ TABLESPOONS SUGAR
- 2½ CLOVES GARLIC
- 1 CUP VINEGAR

ST. ARNOLD'S BEER-INFUSED SAURKRAUT

- ¾ OF 1 ONION, SHREDDED
- 1 HEAD OF GREEN CABBAGE
- ⅛ CUP JUNIPER BERRIES
- ⅛ CUP MUSTARD SEEDS
- ½ TABLESPOON FENUGREEK
- ½ TABLESPOON FENNEL SEEDS
- ¾ CUP WHITE WINE VINEGAR
- ¼ CUP WHITE DISTILLED VINEGAR
- 2-3 BAY LEAVES
- ¼ CUP KOSHER SALT
- ⅛ CUP SUGAR
- 1 BOTTLE ST. ARNOLD BREWING COMPANY'S FANCY LAWNMOWER BEER

serves 4

TO PREPARE THE HOUSE-PICKLED JALAPEÑOS

Combine all ingredients in a pot and boil for 10 minutes. Remove from heat and cool.

TO PREPARE THE SAUERKRAUT

Cut the cabbage on a horizontal bias to a 1½-inch thickness. Cut onions to same thickness. In a bowl, mix the dry spices, juniper berries, mustard seeds, fenugreek and fennel seeds. Top with both vinegars. Set aside. In a small bowl, mix salt and sugar. Sweat the cabbage in a large stockpot. Add the salt and sugar mixture and cook for 4 to 6 minutes. Add the vinegar, dry spices, bay leaves and beer. Cook 20 minutes over medium heat.

TO PREPARE VENISON CHILI

In large pot, heat the butter and oil and sweat the poblano peppers for 20 minutes. Add the venison and beef and cook until brown. Add the tomato paste and the dry spices—cumin to salt and pepper. Stir for 10 minutes, until incorporated. Add the coffee, Lone Star beer and tomatoes. Simmer for 2 hours. In a small bowl, mix the Maseca with just enough water to make a paste. Add to the pot and stir until thickened. Remove from heat.

TO PREPARE THE 'HAUTE' DOGS

Cook the hot dogs on a hot skillet until cooked through. Heat the buns in the oven for 4 minutes.

TO ASSEMBLE

Place the frites in the center of a large plate. Place the hot dog in the bun and balance on top of the frites. Cover with venison chili or sauerkraut. With the venison chili, top with Cotija cheese. With either the venison chili or the sauerkraut, top with pickled jalapeños and crispy onion strings. Garnish with the chervil.

VENISON CHILI

- ⅛ POUND BUTTER
- 1 TABLESPOON BLENDED OIL
- 1¼ POUNDS POBLANO PEPPERS, DICED AND SEEDED
- 1¼ POUNDS JUMBO YELLOW ONIONS, DICED
- 2½ POUNDS BROKEN ARROW RANCH VENISON, GROUND
- 2½ POUNDS GROUND BEEF, 80 PERCENT LEAN
- ¾ CAN TOMATO PASTE
- ¼ CUP CUMIN
- ⅛ CUP GUAJILLO CHILE
- ⅛ CUP ANCHO CHILE
- ⅛ CUP PASILLA
- 1 TABLESPOON ARBOL
- ½ TABLESPOON CAYENNE PEPPER
- SALT AND PEPPER
- 4¼ CUPS COFFEE, DOUBLE STRENGTH
- 2 CANS LONE STAR BEER
- 3 CUPS CANNED WHOLE TOMATOES WITH JUICE
- 1 TABLESPOON MASECA

HAUTE DOG

- 4 HEBREW NATIONAL ALL-BEEF HOT DOGS, 8 OUNCES EACH
- 4 KRAFTSMEN BAKING HOT DOG BUNS
- 24 OUNCES CRISPY FRITES
- 4 OUNCES CRISPY ONION STRINGS
- 2 OUNCES HOUSE-PICKLED JALAPEÑOS
- 2 OUNCES COTIJA MEXICAN CHEESE
- 12 OUNCES VENISON CHILI OR ST. ARNOLD'S BEER-INFUSED SAURKRAUT
- 2 SPRIGS CHERVIL

GREEN BEANS AND GUACAMOLE

MOCKINGBIRD BISTRO

Nestled in Houston's River Oaks neighborhood, Chef John Sheely's Mockingbird Bistro transports guests to a cozy countryside inn, in the heart of the city. The romantic respite is comfortably upscale with wrought-iron chandeliers, exposed brick accents, bistro-tables and floor-to-ceiling windows. Red-velvet barstools, a wrap-around marble counter and an antique bar back—salvaged from Downtown's former Joske's department store—help mark Mockingbird's recently-revamped lounge space. On the restaurant's seasonally-changing menu, Chef Sheely impresses with Texas-influenced-French fare highlighted in current seafood dishes, as well as the flavorful Kobe burger, onion soup and steak frites. For prime people watching and a great view of the neighborhood, request table 14—the most popular spot in the house.

with Provençal tomato ragout and tomato basil vinaigrette

MOCKINGBIRD BISTRO

TO PREPARE TOMATO RAGOUT

In a large saucepan, heat 2 tablespoons olive oil to just before smoking. Carefully add all the tomato ragout ingredients and cook on medium-high heat for several minutes, stirring occasionally, until most of the tomato liquid has evaporated. Tomatoes may char slightly. Season with kosher salt and freshly-ground pepper.

TO PREPARE VINAIGRETTE

In a food processor, blend together the garlic, mustard and vinegar until smooth. Add salt and pepper to taste. With motor running, add oil in a very thin stream and blend until emulsified. Add tomatoes and basil. Vinaigrette may be prepared 4 days ahead and chilled in a tightly-sealed jar. Shake vinaigrette well before serving.

TO PREPARE THE SALMON

Prepare grill or barbecue to medium-high heat. Brush salmon with remaining 2 tablespoons oil and sprinkle with salt and pepper. Grill salmon until just opaque in center, about 4 minutes per side. Place tomato ragout on plate and top with salmon, then top salmon with tomato basil vinaigrette.

4	WILD SALMON FILLETS, 8 OUNCES EACH
	KOSHER SALT
	FRESHLY-GROUND BLACK PEPPER

TOMATO RAGOUT

6	LARGE ROMA TOMATOES, PEELED, SEEDED AND COARSELY-CHOPPED
4	TABLESPOONS EXTRA VIRGIN OLIVE OIL
2	TEASPOONS RED WINE VINEGAR
¼	CUP BASIL LEAVES, JULIENNED
10	KALAMATA OLIVES
1	LARGE SHALLOT, JULIENNED
1	TABLESPOON CAPERS, DRAINED
2	GARLIC CLOVES, MINCED

TOMATO BASIL VINAIGRETTE

3	GARLIC CLOVES, MINCED
2	TEASPOONS DIJON MUSTARD
½	CUP RED WINE VINEGAR
6	BASIL LEAVES, JULIENNED
1½	CUPS PLUS 2 TABLESPOONS EXTRA VIRGIN OLIVE OIL
3	CUPS VINE-RIPENED RED TEARDROP TOMATOES, HALVED
3	CUPS VINE-RIPENED YELLOW TEARDROP TOMATOES, HALVED

serves 4

FLOURLESS CHOCOLATE CAKE
MOCKINGBIRD BISTRO

7	OUNCES SEMI-SWEET CHOCOLATE, CHOPPED
200	GRAMS BUTTER
1	CUP SUGAR
4	EGGS, WHITES AND YOLKS SEPARATED

serves 8

Preheat oven to 350°F.

Line 1, 9-inch round pan with wax paper. In a bowl, beat egg yolks and ½ cup sugar. In a double boiler or a metal bowl, set over a saucepan of simmering water, melt the chocolate and the butter, stirring until smooth. Remove from heat and fold in the egg yolks. In a bowl, beat the egg whites until frothy. Add the remaining sugar and beat until stiff. Fold egg whites into the chocolate mixture. Fill the baking pan and place in a water bath. Bake for 40 minutes. Cool on a rack and then chill.

NOTE: Serve chilled and accompany with ice cream, if desired.

OLIVETTE

GREEN BEANS AND GUACAMOLE

Located on an 18-acre wooded oasis—inside The Houstonian Hotel—Olivette remains an under-the-radar culinary jewel, set in the heart of the Galleria area. The lushly-landscaped property is an escape within the city. At Olivette, Tuscan styling and stunning views of the Houstonian's nature-filled grounds impart a warmly-inviting ambiance, while a lively display kitchen affords diners a view behind the scenes. On the seasonally-changing menu, Mediterranean-influenced American cuisine delights in dishes like the bouillabaisse with garlic rouille and a tomato-saffron broth. The Liberty Farms duck breast is also a standout, which arrives alongside vegetable fricassee, fingerling potatoes and a shallot sauce. Save room for dessert.

BROTH

1/3	CUP OLIVE OIL
1	CUP SHRIMP SHELLS
2	LOBSTER HEADS, CLEANED AND RINSED
1	YELLOW ONION, COARSELY CHOPPED
1	CARROT, COARSELY CHOPPED
2	CELERY STALKS, COARSELY CHOPPED
1	FENNEL BULB, COARSELY CHOPPED
1	LEEK, WHITE AND LIGHT GREEN PARTS, COARSELY CHOPPED AND SOAKED IN WATER
	ZEST OF 10 LEMONS
6	GARLIC CLOVES
2	CUPS ROMA TOMATOES, COARSELY CHOPPED
1/4	CUP BRANDY
1	CUP VERMOUTH
3	QUARTS WATER
1	MEDIUM SIZE FISH BONE
2	BAY LEAVES
1	TEASPOON DRIED THYME

FINES HERBS

1/4	CUP TARRAGON, FINELY CHOPPED
1/4	CUP CHERVIL, FINELY CHOPPED
1/4	CUP CHIVES, FINELY CHOPPED
1/4	CUP PARSLEY, FINELY CHOPPED

Preheat oven to 250°F.

TO PREPARE THE BROTH

In a pot large enough to hold all of the ingredients, heat the olive oil to the smoke point. Add the shrimp shells and lobster heads and roast until fragrant, making sure not to burn. Add the next 5 ingredients and roast until caramelized. Add the lemon zest, garlic and tomatoes and cook until almost dry. Deglaze with the brandy first and reduce for 2 minutes. Then add the vermouth and reduce for another 2 minutes. Add the next 4 ingredients, bring to a boil and then reduce heat and simmer for 1 hour. Strain into another pot and continue to simmer until reduced to approximately 1 quart. Reserve.

TO PREPARE THE ROUILLE

Scoop out half of the potato into a blender. Save the other half for later use. Add remaining ingredients except for the olive oil. Turn on the blender and slowly incorporate the oil to make an emulsion while the motor is running. Season with salt.

TO PREPARE THE TOMATO CONFIT

Combine all ingredients in a pan and put in the oven for 8 minutes or until tomato skins begin to break down. Set aside to cool. To use tomato confit in the bouillabaisse, lift the tomatoes out of the oil bath with a slotted spoon. Reserve oil for another use, such as dipping bread.

TO PREPARE THE FINES HERBS

In a small bowl, combine all ingredients. Set aside.

TO PREPARE THE BOUILLABAISSE

Season the scallops and fish and sear both sides in a large, heavy-bottomed pan. Deglaze with the bouillabaisse broth. Add the shellfish, shrimp, tomato confit and leeks. Simmer uncovered until the clams and mussels open. Add the calamari and cook for 1 minute. Adjust the seasoning and add the butter and fines herbs. Spread 1 tablespoon of the rouille on each slice of ciabatta. Divide the bouillabaisse into 4 bowls and garnish each one with a piece of ciabatta.

STEW

12	SHRIMP, DEVEINED
4	LARGE SCALLOPS
20	MUSSELS, SCRUBBED
12	MANILA CLAMS, SCRUBBED
5	CALAMARI
4	CHILEAN SEA BASS FILLETS, 3 OUNCES EACH
2	LEEKS, WHITE AND LIGHT GREEN PARTS, CUT INTO RINGS AND SOAKED IN WATER
1	CUP GRAPE TOMATO CONFIT, SEE RECIPE
4	TABLESPOONS SAFFRON ROUILLE, SEE RECIPE
4	SLICES CIABATTA BREAD, TOASTED JUST BEFORE SERVING
1	TEASPOON FINES HERBS, SEE RECIPE
1	TABLESPOON WHOLE BUTTER, SOFTENED

ROUILLE

1	SMALL RUSSET POTATO, BAKED AND COOLED
3	CLOVES GARLIC, ROASTED
1	PINCH SAFFRON
1	EGG YOLK
1	TABLESPOON BOUILLABAISSE BROTH
1/3	CUP OLIVE OIL
	SALT

TOMATO CONFIT

1	PINT GRAPE TOMATOES
1	QUART OLIVE OIL
3	SPRIGS THYME
2	BAY LEAVES
1	TEASPOON WHOLE PEPPERCORN
3	GARLIC CLOVES

serves 4

SOUTHWEST CAESAR SALAD

OLIVETTE

SOUTHWEST CAESAR DRESSING

1	EGG YOLK
1	TABLESPOON GARLIC, MINCED
1	TEASPOON DIJON MUSTARD
1	TO 2 ANCHOVY FILLETS, MINCED
¼	TEASPOON SALT
½	TEASPOON CUMIN, GROUND
½	TEASPOON CORIANDER, GROUND
½	TEASPOON WORCESTERSHIRE SAUCE
2	TABLESPOONS COLD WATER
½	CUP CANOLA OIL
½	CUP OLIVE OIL
1	TABLESPOON SAMBAL CHILI PASTE
½	TEASPOON LIME JUICE
½	TEASPOON LEMON JUICE
1½	TABLESPOONS PARMESAN CHEESE, FINELY GRATED

SALAD

3	CUPS ROMAINE LETTUCE, CUT INTO 1½-INCH PIECES, WASHED AND DRIED, LOOSELY PACKED
½	CUP SOUTHWEST CAESAR DRESSING
3	TABLESPOONS BLACK BEANS, COOKED
3	TABLESPOONS ROASTED CORN KERNELS
2	TABLESPOONS PUMPKIN SEEDS, ROASTED, DIVIDED
3	TABLESPOONS COTIJA CHEESE, CRUMBLED, DIVIDED
1	CUP TORTILLA STRIPS, CRISPED IN OVEN OR FRIED LIGHTLY IN OIL, DIVIDED

serves 4

TO PREPARE THE SALAD DRESSING

Combine first 9 ingredients in a food processor—egg yolk to water. Process until smooth, then slowly add canola and olive oil—drop-by-drop—and increase the flow as the emulsion forms. When oils are incorporated and the mixture is smooth, add remaining ingredients and pulse until smooth. Yields about 2½ cups and can be refrigerated for up to 1 week.

TO PREPARE THE SALAD

In a large bowl, toss the lettuce with the dressing, beans, corn, half of the pumpkin seeds, Cotija cheese and tortilla strips. Mix well and season to taste with salt and pepper. Divide the salad onto 4 chilled plates and sprinkle with the remaining pumpkin seeds, cheese and tortilla strips. Serve immediately.

GREEN BEANS AND GUACAMOLE

OUISIE'S TABLE

Venturing into River Oaks' Ouisie's Table feels a lot like a visit to a close friend's house—and it should. Native Houstonian Elouise Adams Jones—better known to locals as Ouisie—opened the upscale Southern restaurant in 1973 as a way to share family-style dishes from her childhood. Set inside a renovated country house, Ouisie's features multi-room dining spaces that are cozy and intimate, boasting fireplaces, high-ceilings, garden views and a blackboard advertising the day's specials. Other highlights include Lucy's Porch—an air-conditioned patio space—and Cooper's Bin, a private wine cellar with seating for 14. On the menu, Ouisie's assortment of regionally-inspired dishes reflect her love for the Gulf Coast and elegant Louisiana cuisine. The southern shrimp and grits remain a local favorite, as does the chicken

GREEN BEANS A

TO PREPARE THE DEVILED EGGS

Put the eggs in a pan and cover with water. Bring to a boil over medium heat. Boil for 15 minutes. Drain the eggs and shake them around in the pan to break the shells. Fill the pan with cold water and let everything sit until the eggs are room temperature. Eggs will peel easily this way. After peeling the eggs, pat dry and slice each in half. Carefully remove the yellow yolk without tearing the white part. Place yolks on a dinner plate and set the white halves on another plate. Mash the yolks using a dinner fork. Add 2-3 tablespoons mayonnaise and 2 teaspoons Dijon mustard, a dash of salt and a grind of pepper. Combine all until smooth. With a small spoon or small spatula carefully fill each egg-white half with the yolk filling. Garnish top with a leaf of parsley or cilantro, a sprinkle of cayenne pepper or a few capers.

TO SERVE

Toss chilled greens and cabbage with olive oil, lemon juice and sea salt. Place lettuce leaves on a large plate to provide a frame for the salad. Place the lump crabmeat on top of the dressed greens and top with rémoulade, reserving some sauce to serve on the side. Arrange the other components around it with the deviled eggs on the edge of the plate. Serve with crisp crostini, saltine crackers or hot, buttered biscuits. Garnish with lemon wedges.

CRAB COBB SALAD

2 LARGE LETTUCE LEAVES, GREEN TIP OR ROMAINE

3 OUNCES JUMBO LUMP CRABMEAT, CHILLED

EQUAL PARTS BABY ARUGULA, RED TIP LETTUCE AND THINLY-SHREDDED CABBAGE, COMBINED TO MAKE 2 CUPS, WASHED, PREPPED AND CHILLED

1 TABLESPOON EXTRA VIRGIN OLIVE OIL, COMBINED WITH A SQUEEZE OF LEMON AND A DASH OF SEA SALT

1 SLICE BACON, COOKED CRISP AND CRUMBLED

6 YELLOW AND RED CHERRY OR PEAR TOMATOES, HALVED AND CHILLED

½ RIPE AVOCADO

½ LIME, JUICED

¼ TO ½ FRESH JALAPEÑO, MINCED

1 TABLESPOON WHITE ONION, MINCED

SALT

DEVILED EGGS, SEE RECIPE

RÉMOULADE SAUCE, SEE APPENDIX

CROSTINI, SALTINE CRACKERS OR HOT BUTTERED BISCUITS, FOR SERVING

LEMON WEDGES

DEVILED EGGS

4 EGGS

2 TO 3 TABLESPOONS MAYONNAISE

2 TEASPOONS DIJON MUSTARD

SALT AND PEPPER

CAYENNE PEPPERS OR A FEW CAPERS, FOR GARNISH

serves 1

FRIED OYSTERS

LARGE BOTTLE CANOLA OIL, FOR FRYING

2 DOZEN OYSTERS

1 QUART BUTTERMILK

CORN FLOUR AND CORN MEAL

SALT AND PEPPER

RED SAUCE

2 CUPS KETCHUP

2 TABLESPOONS LEMON JUICE

2 TABLESPOONS WORCESTERSHIRE SAUCE

1 TABLESPOON TABASCO SAUCE

1 TABLESPOON PREPARED HORSERADISH

serves 8 appetizer portions

TO PREPARE RED SAUCE
Combine all ingredients in a bowl. Adjust according to taste. Set aside. Makes 1 pint.

TO PREPARE FRIED OYSTERS
Heat oil in fry daddy or deep pot to 350°F. Do not fry at temperature lower than 350°F. Drain oysters well and place in shallow dish with buttermilk. Remove one at a time and dredge in 1 part corn flour to 3 parts corn meal seasoned with salt and pepper. Place coated oysters on a plate without stacking. Fry at 350°F until crispy and brown. Do not crowd, as oysters need space to crisp all over. When done, remove to drain on paper towels. Serve immediately with a lemon wedge and red sauce.

NOTE: People can wait. Oysters can't. Eat them when hot.

PAPPAS RESTAURANTS

GREEN BEANS AND GUACAMOLE

In 1897, H.D. Pappas left Greece to pursue his restaurateur dreams in America—paving the way for his family's future dining ventures throughout the United States. Although H.D.'s sons, Pete and Jim, initially opted for a career path in the restaurant equipment-supply business, the two eventually decided to try their hand in the restaurant field, opening two Dot Coffee Shops and a Brisket House—now known as Pappas Bar-B-Q—in Houston. Today, Jim's sons, Harris and Chris, operate the company's more than 80 restaurant concepts—from Arizona to Ohio—including the popular Pappas Bros. Steakhouse, Pappadeaux Seafood Kitchen, Pappasito's Cantina, Pappas Burger and Yia Yia Mary's Greek Kitchen.

Preheat oven to 275°F.

Place 6, 4½-inch by 1¼-inch buttered baking rings on a parchment-lined baking sheet. Spray with nonstick spray, then line the baking rings with parchment paper cut into 14-inch by 2-inch strips. In a food processor, pulse chocolate chunks and macadamia nuts until coarsely ground. Place dark brown sugar and hot melted butter in the bowl of a stand mixer with a paddle attachment. Mix on medium speed for 5 minutes. Drizzle in extract and add in eggs 1 at a time. Once all of the eggs have been added, stop the mixer and scrape the sides and bottom of the bowl. Return mixer to medium speed and continue mixing for 5 minutes. In a separate bowl, sift flour, baking powder and salt together. Turn mixer to low and slowly add sifted ingredients. Mix for 10 seconds, stop and scrape the sides and bottom of the bowl.

Continue to mix on low for 2 more minutes. Add coarse ground chocolate/macadamia nut mixture, mix for 20 seconds or until nut and chocolate is dispersed throughout the batter. Pour batter into prepared baking rings and bake for 40 to 45 minutes, or until a cake tester comes out clean. Cool to room temperature before removing rings. Once completely cooled, remove rings from the blonde brownie.

TO PREPARE THE CARAMEL SAUCE
Combine granulated sugar, water, light syrup and lemon juice in a saucepot over medium heat. Bring just up to a boil, then lower heat. Simmer until caramel turns medium brown to amber in color. Remove from heat and very slowly whisk in heavy cream, as whisking too fast will cause the caramel to overflow. Pour into a container, cover and allow to cool.

TO PREPARE THE CHOCOLATE SAUCE
Combine unsalted butter and water in a saucepot over medium heat. Once butter has melted, add chocolate chips, sugar and light syrup. Bring to a boil, stirring to thoroughly incorporate. Reduce heat to low and simmer until chocolate is smooth. Remove from heat and stir in vanilla extract. Strain chocolate sauce through a fine mesh sieve and allow to cool.

TO SERVE
Place a warm brownie in the center of a dish and top with scoop of ice cream. Drizzle with caramel sauce and chocolate sauce.

NOTE:
Chocolate sauce recipe yields approximately 1 cup. Caramel sauce yields approximately 1½ cups.

BROWNIES

1¼	CUPS SEMI-SWEET CHOCOLATE CHUNKS
¾	CUP TOASTED MACADAMIA NUTS, WHOLE
1	POUND DARK BROWN SUGAR
6	OUNCES UNSALTED BUTTER, MELTED AND HOT
2½	TABLESPOONS VANILLA EXTRACT
2	EGGS
2	CUPS ALL-PURPOSE FLOUR
1½	TEASPOONS BAKING POWDER
½	TEASPOON SALT
	CARAMEL SAUCE
	CHOCOLATE SAUCE

CARAMEL SAUCE

1¼	CUPS GRANULATED SUGAR
3	TABLESPOONS WATER
3	TABLESPOONS LIGHT KARO SYRUP
½	TEASPOON FRESH LEMON JUICE
1	CUP HEAVY CREAM

CHOCOLATE SAUCE

4½	OUNCES UNSALTED BUTTER
6	TABLESPOONS WATER
¼	POUND SEMI-SWEET CHOCOLATE CHUNKS
½	CUP GRANULATED SUGAR
2½	TABLESPOONS LIGHT KARO SYRUP
¾	TEASPOON VANILLA EXTRACT

makes 6 brownies

CAJETA

CAJETA

2	CUPS VANILLA ICE CREAM
⅓	CUP TOASTED COCONUT AND PECAN COATING
3	TABLESPOONS CARAMEL SAUCE
1	TABLESPOON CHOCOLATE SAUCE
1	TABLESPOON WHIPPED CREAM
	STRAWBERRIES
	MINT
	CINNAMON

TOASTED COCONUT AND PECAN COATING

½	POUND SNOWFLAKE COCONUT
¼	POUND MEDIUM PECAN PIECES

CARAMEL SAUCE

1¼	CUPS GRANULATED SUGAR
3	TABLESPOONS WATER
3	TABLESPOONS LIGHT KARO SYRUP
½	TEASPOON FRESH LEMON JUICE
1	CUP HEAVY CREAM

CHOCOLATE SAUCE

4½	OUNCES UNSALTED BUTTER
6	TABLESPOONS WATER
¼	POUND SEMI-SWEET CHOCOLATE CHIPS, HIGH QUALITY
½	CUP GRANULATED SUGAR
2½	TABLESPOONS LIGHT KARO SYRUP
¾	TEASPOON VANILLA EXTRACT

WHIPPED CREAM

1	CUP HEAVY CREAM
¼	CUP GRANULATED SUGAR

serves 2

TO PREPARE THE COCONUT AND PECAN COATING
Preheat oven to 350°F. Place snowflake coconut and pecan pieces on two separate metal sheet pans with sides. Toast until golden brown, stirring mixture occasionally to ensure even browning. Remove from oven and allow to cool on sheet pan. Once completely cool, place toasted coconut and pecan pieces in a large mixing bowl.

TO PREPARE THE CARAMEL SAUCE
Combine granulated sugar, water, light syrup and lemon juice in a saucepot over medium heat. Bring just up to a boil then lower heat. Simmer until caramel turns medium brown to amber in color. Remove from heat and very slowly whisk in heavy cream, as whisking too fast will cause the caramel to overflow. Pour into container with lid and allow to cool.

TO PREPARE THE CHOCOLATE SAUCE
Combine unsalted butter and water in a saucepot over medium heat. Once butter has melted, add chocolate chips, sugar and light syrup. Bring to a boil, stirring to thoroughly incorporate. Reduce heat to low and simmer until chocolate is smooth. Remove from heat and stir in vanilla extract. Strain chocolate sauce through a fine mesh sieve and allow to cool.

TO PREPARE THE WHIPPED CREAM
Whisk heavy cream and granulated sugar in a mixing bowl until the cream holds stiff peaks. Store in refrigerator until needed, but must be used the same day.

TO SERVE
To make the Cajeta, scoop into 4 equal balls, about ½ cup. Roll the balls in toasted coconut and pecan coating, covering the ice cream entirely. Stack the Cajetas in the center of the plate. Pour 3 tablespoons caramel sauce directly on top. Drizzle 1 tablespoon chocolate sauce on and around the Cajetas. Garnish with whipped cream, strawberry and mint. Lightly dust with cinnamon.

PHILIPPE
RESTAURANT + LOUNGE

GREEN BEANS AND GUACAMOLE

Parisian-trained Chef Philippe Schmit—Houston's "French Cowboy"—brings the Uptown area eclectic French fare with a Texas twist at his BLVD Place restaurant. His two-story Philippe Restaurant + Lounge opened in early 2011 and has been a popular destination among the well-heeled ever since. In the first floor lounge, fresh-faced professionals unwind on wrap-around banquettes with post-work cocktails and light bites. Upstairs, the rustic-chic decor is marked by black-and-white trompe l'oeil wallpaper, butcher-block tables and antique mirror accents. On the menu, Chef Philippe shines with the spicy duck confit tamales, Burgundy beef cheeks and baked scallops. For a memorable meal, reserve the Chef's Table—along with your 15 nearest and dearest—and enjoy one of Chef Philippe's exclusive specialty menus.

TO PREPARE THE BÉCHAMEL

In a large stockpot, melt the butter and flour over medium heat. Whisk for 2 to 3 minutes. Add milk and cook for 10 minutes, until smooth, stirring continuously. Remove from heat and mix in cheese, nutmeg, yolks, salt and pepper. Set aside.

TO PREPARE THE JULIENNE VEGETABLES

Sauté julienned vegetables with olive oil until tender. Remove from heat and add salt and pepper to taste. Add basil julienne. Set aside.

TO PREPARE THE SCALLOPS

In a non-stick pan over medium heat, sear scallops with olive oil until golden brown, about 2 minutes. Remove the scallops from the pan and deglaze with whiskey. Add the veal demi glace. Set aside.

TO SERVE

Top scallops with béchamel and bread crumbs. Broil until browned. Using a fork, twirl julienne of vegetables as if spaghetti and place on a plate, forming 3 piles. Place scallops on plate, leaving a space between scallops and vegetables. Spoon whiskey demi glace down the middle.

SCALLOPS

3	SCALLOPS
½	CUP VEAL DEMI GLACE
½	TABLESPOON WHISKEY, PREFERABLY JACK DANIELS
2	OUNCES BÉCHAMEL SAUCE
4	OUNCES JULIENNE VEGETABLES

BÉCHAMEL SAUCE

1	CUP WHOLE MILK
½	OUNCE BUTTER
½	OUNCE FLOUR
½	OUNCE EGG YOLKS
¼	OUNCE GRUYÉRE CHEESE
½	TABLESPOON BREAD CRUMBS
	PINCH OF NUTMEG
	SALT AND WHITE PEPPER

JULIENNE VEGETABLES

2	OUNCES CARROTS, JULIENNED AND BLANCHED
2	OUNCES PARSNIPS, JULIENNED AND BLANCHED
2	OUNCES ZUCCHINI, JULIENNED AND BLANCHED
¾	TABLESPOON OLIVE OIL
1	OUNCE BASIL, JULIENNED
	SALT AND PEPPER

serves 1

GREEN BEANS AND GUACAMOLE

CRISPY RICE PAPER SALMON

SALMON

4	SALMON FILLETS, LOIN CUT, 7 OUNCES EACH
	RICE PAPER
2	EGGS, BEATEN
1¾	POUNDS SPAGHETTI SQUASH
4	TABLESPOONS SCALLIONS, SLICED
4	OUNCES WHITE SOY SAUCE
4	PINCHES OF BASIL CHIFFONADE
4	PINCHES OF CHERVIL

VEGETABLE BRUNOISE

2	OUNCES ZUCCHINI, JULIENNED, DICED AND BLANCHED
2	OUNCES YELLOW SQUASH, JULIENNED, DICED AND BLANCHED
2	OUNCES TOMATOES, DICED
2	OUNCES BUTTERNUT SQUASH, JULIENNED, DICED AND BLANCHED

VIERGE VINAIGRETTE

6	TABLESPOONS OLIVE OIL
1	LEMON, ZESTED AND JUICED
2	TABLESPOONS SHERRY VINEGAR
	SALT AND PEPPER

BROCCOLI BASIL PESTO

4	OUNCES BROCCOLI, COARSELY PURÉED
4	OUNCES BASIL, BLANCHED
4	TABLESPOONS OLIVE OIL
2	OUNCES PARMESAN CHEESE
1	OUNCE PINE NUTS

serves 4

Preheat oven to 350°F.

TO PREPARE THE SPAGHETTI SQUASH
Cut the spaghetti squash in half, wrap in foil and roast for 20 to 30 minutes. Remove from oven and set aside. When cool, scrape flesh into a bowl.

TO PREPARE THE VEGETABLE BRUNOISE
Combine all ingredients in a bowl and set aside.

TO PREPARE THE VINAIGRETTE
In a mixing bowl, whisk together the lemon juice and sherry vinegar. Add olive oil in a slow stream until emulsified. Add lemon zest, salt and pepper. Set aside.

TO PREPARE THE BROCCOLI BASIL PESTO
In a small food processor or using a mortar and pestle, combine the basil, olive oil, Parmesan and pine nuts. Transfer to a bowl. Blanch the broccoli, purée it and add to the bowl. Set aside.

TO PREPARE THE SALMON
In a non-stick pan, heat 1 tablespoon of olive and sear the salmon. Set aside. In a small bowl add a splash of water to the beaten eggs to make a wash. Brush the egg wash over the rice paper. Using 2 overlapping leaves for each loin, place salmon on paper. Spread approximately 2 ounces of the pesto over the salmon. Roll salmon in the paper, keeping it snug like a sushi roll. Repeat for all salmon loins. Heat 1 tablespoon of olive oil over medium heat and sear the paper-wrapped salmon until golden on all sides. At the same time, sauté spaghetti squash in a splash of olive oil. Add scallions, salt and pepper to taste. To finish add white soy sauce.

TO SERVE
Using a round mold, place the spaghetti squash in the middle of plate, cut 1 salmon roll into 3 medallions and place across from the spaghetti squash. Combine brunoise vegetables, basil chiffonade, chervil and vierge vinaigrette. Spoon around the salmon.

NOTE: Brunoise means to julienne and then dice.

PIATTO RISTORANTE

John Marion Carrabba carries on the Carrabba family tradition of turning out home-style Italian cuisine at his two, Houston-born Piatto Ristorante locations. The contemporary dining concept, which opened more than a decade ago, showcases an array of made-from-scratch dishes, some centered on recipes that date back four generations. Pastas, pizzas, soups and salads line Piatto's menu, along with grilled meat and seafood selections. Signature standouts include the stuffed shrimp and asparagus speciali, the latter of which arrives lightly-breaded, fried and topped with jumbo lump crabmeat. In addition to the regular menu, Piatto offers catering by Carrabba's mother, Mary Ann Carrabba, who's known to turn out a range of cuisines from Italian to Mexican to American.

GREEN BEANS AND GUACAMOLE

BOLOGNESE SAUCE

½	CUP EXTRA VIRGIN OLIVE OIL
½	ONION, FINELY CHOPPED
2	GARLIC CLOVES, CRUSHED
12	OUNCES GROUND BEEF
8	OUNCES GROUND PORK
½	TEASPOON DRIED OREGANO
½	TEASPOON BLACK PEPPER
½	TEASPOON COARSE SALT
6	TABLESPOONS RED WINE
¼	CUP CELERY
6	CUPS TOMATO SAUCE, SEE APPENDIX
8	SERVINGS PASTA
	PARMESAN, GRATED, FOR SERVING

serves 8

In a food processor, finely chop celery, onions and garlic. Heat extra virgin olive oil in a sauté pan over medium heat. Add celery, onions and garlic, and sauté until softened and translucent. Add meat, salt, black pepper and oregano, and stir thoroughly over medium heat for 15 minutes. Strain the meat in a colander and then return to sauté pan and add wine, cooking over medium heat. Reduce for approximately 2 minutes. Add tomato sauce and simmer, stirring frequently, for 5 to 10 minutes. Serve with pasta and freshly-grated Parmesan.

NOTE: Bolognese can be refrigerated for up to 3 days and frozen up to 1 month.

CEVICHE
PIATTO RISTORANTE

1	CUP JUMBO SHRIMP, COOKED AND CHOPPED INTO ½-INCH CUBES
¾	CUP TOMATOES, DICED
1	BUNCH CILANTRO, CHOPPED
1	LARGE JALAPEÑO, DICED SMALL
4	MEDIUM AVOCADOS
½	CUP YELLOW ONION
½	TABLESPOON COARSE SALT
¼	TABLESPOON BLACK PEPPER
2	TABLESPOONS VODKA
¼	TABLESPOON HORSERADISH
¼	TABLESPOON TABASCO
¾	CUP LEMON JUICE
12	OUNCES KETCHUP

serves 4

Chop avocados into ¾-inch cubes and soak in a bowl with lemon juice for 15 minutes. In a large bowl, add tomatoes, onions and jalapeños, salt and pepper. Add shrimp, cilantro, ketchup, Tabasco, horseradish and vodka and mix well. Lift the avocados out of the lemon juice and add to the ceviche.

TO SERVE:
Place ceviche in lettuce-lined martini glass. Serve with tortilla chips.

GREEN BEANS AND GUACAMOLE

QUATTRO

GREEN BEANS AND GUACAMOLE

Situated on the third floor of Downtown's Four Seasons Hotel, Quattro takes its name from the restaurant's four "faces"—breakfast, lunch, dinner and a lively antipasto bar. There, Chef Maurizio Ferrarese delights with his vibrant Italian dishes, culled from his native Italy. Much-loved offerings like the prosciutto flatbread and veal Milanese remain steadfast on the seasonally-changing menu, as do a mix of risotto dishes inspired by Maurizio's native Piedmont region. Pair them with an Italian vino from Quattro's well-executed wine list. Looking to break away from tradition? Chef Maurizio, who often makes the rounds to greet diners, is happy to create a custom tasting menu for guests.

FOR THE ASPARAGUS PURÉE
In a pan, sauté shallots with olive oil over medium heat. Add chopped asparagus and cover with water. Boil for about 6 minutes. Remove from heat and cool. Purée in a blender until smooth and thick. Set aside.

FOR THE CRAB
In a bowl, combine the crabmeat with a dill, lemon juice and lemon zest, to taste. Add some asparagus shavings and a tomato petal.

FOR RISOTTO
In a saucepan, melt half the butter and sweat the onion without coloring. Add the rice and stir for 2 to 3 minutes. Add enough water to just cover the rice and season lightly with salt. Add the asparagus purée. Continue to stir gently as the rice begins to absorb the liquid, add more water as necessary. Boil for 5 minutes. Add the diced asparagus. The rice will take approximately 15 minutes to cook and must remain al dente. Taste the rice to check the firmness. When ready, remove from heat and add 2 ounces of butter and a spoon of olive oil. Stir well and finish with 2 ounces of Parmigiano. Taste for seasoning.

TO SERVE
Pour the risotto into the center of a large bowl. Place the crab mix on the risotto.

6	OUNCES RISOTTO VIALONE NANO OR CARNAROLI
2	OUNCES ONION BRUNOISE
4	OUNCES PLUS 2 OUNCES BUTTER
2	OUNCES DICED ASPARAGUS
4	OUNCES PLUS 2 OUNCES PARMIGIANO, GRATED
4	OUNCES JUMBO CRAB
	EXTRA VIRGIN OLIVE OIL
7½	CUPS BOILING WATER
1	LEMON, JUICED AND ZESTED
	DILL, TO TASTE

GREEN ASPARAGUS PURÉE

2	SHALLOTS
	OLIVE OIL
12	OUNCES ASPARAGUS, DICED

serves 2

VEAL & VITELLO TONNATO

QUATTRO

2	VEAL FILETS, APPROXIMATELY 1 POUND
15	OUNCES TUNA, GRADE 1 OR TUNA GRADE
1	TEASPOON CAPERS, PLUS MORE FOR GARNISH
3	ANCHOVY FILLETS, PLUS MORE FOR GARNISH
1¼	CUPS EXTRA VIRGIN OLIVE OIL
2	BAY LEAVES
3	TABLESPOONS DRY WHITE WINE
1	EGG YOLK, PASTEURIZED
	SALT AND PEPPER
10	BLACK PEPPERCORNS
½	CUP SALAD GREENS
½	LEMON
½	TEASPOON MALDON SALT, FOR GARNISH

serves 4

TO PREPARE THE SAUCE

Chop 5 ounces of tuna into cubes and place in a pot. Cover with extra virgin olive oil, about ¾ cup. Add 2 bay leaves and 10 black peppercorns. Cook at low temperature for 8 minutes or until cooked through. Remove from heat and drain. Cool in an ice water bath, pat dry and place in a blender. Add the capers, anchovies and white wine. Blend until creamy, adding a touch of water, if necessary. In the meantime, whisk the egg yolk with a teaspoon of warm water until well blended. Slowly add ½ cup of extra virgin olive, initially in drops and then in a stream, whisking to emulsify and thicken. Squeeze lemon into the mayonnaise, extracting most of the juice. Season with salt and pepper. Combine the tuna mixture with the mayo to reach a creamy consistency.

TO PREPARE THE VEAL AND TUNA

Clean the veal filet, removing all fat and silver skin. Wrap it in plastic wrap and shape it like salami. Place in a steamer insert, over a pot of boiling water, for about 10 minutes or until it reaches an internal temperature of 125°F, for medium rare. Remove from heat and cool. Slice thin and season with Maldon salt and drizzle with olive oil. Quickly pan sear the tuna, keeping it rare.

TO SERVE

Plate it alternating the veal and the tuna. Top with sauce and garnish with capers, anchovies and greens.

RAINBOW LODGE

Set along the banks of the White Oak Bayou, inside a more than 100
log cabin, the Rainbow Lodge remains one of the city's most-loved an
dining destinations. Inside the converted Heights' home, stone firepl
heads and antler-clad chandeliers adorn the multi-room restaurant, l
the lodge's cozy appeal. Outside, tables line a dramatic deck, which ov
the restaurant's tropical grounds and makes a serene escape. On the c
front, wild game and seafood reign supreme, highlighted by standout
slow-smoked duck and andouille sausage gumbo and pan-seared red s
Don't miss Rainbow Lodge's award-winning wine selection, highlight
monthly patio wine series, as well as the "Grand Food and Wine Pairi
held in the spring and fall.

SOUTHERN FRIED QUAIL ON CHEESY GRITS
with bourbon bacon cream gravy

RAINBOW LODGE

TO PREPARE THE GRITS

Place the milk, cream, water and salt into a large, heavy-bottomed pot over medium-high heat and bring to a boil. Once the milk mixture comes to a boil, gradually add the grits, whisking continually. Once incorporated, decrease the heat to low and cover. Remove lid and whisk frequently—every 3 to 4 minutes—to prevent grits from sticking or forming lumps, making sure to get into corners of pot when whisking. Cook for 40 to 45 minutes or until mixture is creamy. Remove from the heat, add the pepper and butter and whisk to combine. Once the butter melts, gradually whisk in the cheese a little at a time.

TO PREPARE QUAIL

Pour buttermilk into a bowl. Season the quail halves with salt and pepper and place in the bowl with the buttermilk. Marinate for 1 hour. In a shallow bowl, mix the flour, salt, pepper and cayenne. Heat the peanut oil over medium-high heat to 360°F in a large, heavy skillet, preferably cast iron. Drain the quail, discarding the buttermilk and place in the seasoned flour. Toss gently to coat evenly. Slide the quail, in batches, into the hot oil and cook about 4 to 5 minutes, per side, or until the quail are done and golden brown. Remove and drain on layers of paper towels. Keep warm.

TO PREPARE THE GRAVY

Brown bacon in a heavy skillet until it starts to crisp, about 5 to 6 minutes. Skillet can be the same one used for the quail. Stir in shallots and flour until well-blended and cook over medium heat for 3 to 4 minutes, until the flour is bubbly and turning golden brown. Carefully add whiskey, as the alcohol will flame up, then whisk in stock and reduce by half. Add cream and boil until thick and smooth, stirring constantly. Add butter, whisking to incorporate, and season with salt and pepper.

TO SERVE

Spoon ½ cup of grits onto the center of a warmed plate, place the fried quail on top of the grits. Pour gravy over the quail. Garnish with chopped green onions.

QUAIL

8	SEMI-BONELESS QUAIL
	SALT AND GROUND BLACK PEPPER
1½	CUPS BUTTERMILK
1½	CUPS ALL-PURPOSE FLOUR
1	TEASPOON SALT
½	TEASPOON GROUND BLACK PEPPER
¼	TEASPOON CAYENNE
2	CUPS PEANUT OIL
½	BUNCH GREEN ONIONS, CHOPPED

CHEESY GRITS

2	CUPS WHOLE MILK
1	CUP HEAVY CREAM
1	CUP WATER
1½	TEASPOONS SALT
1	CUP HOMESTEAD GRISTMILL WHITE CORN GRITS
½	TEASPOON FRESHLY GROUND BLACK PEPPER
4	TABLESPOONS UNSALTED BUTTER
4	OUNCES WHITE CHEDDAR, GRATED

BOURBON BACON CREAMY GRAVY

4	SLICES APPLE-SMOKED BACON, DICED
¼	CUP SHALLOTS, MINCED
2	TABLESPOONS FLOUR
¼	CUP BOURBON WHISKEY
1	CUP CHICKEN STOCK
½	CUP HEAVY CREAM
1	TABLESPOON BUTTER
	SALT AND PEPPER

serves 8

RAY'S GOURMET COUNTRY

GREEN BEANS AND GUACAMOLE

There aren't any can openers hiding in the kitchen of Ray's Gourmet Country. All food used at the refined, Fulshear-set restaurant are drawn from local markets, found at nearby farms or made-from-scratch. In fact, the proximity to producers was a key factor in helping restaurateur Ray Salti and Denmark-born-chef, Soren Pedersen, select a location. Inside, the contemporary space is simple and sleek with scored concrete floors, wood accents and an open kitchen highlighted by a black-and-white photomural that hangs overhead. Chef Soren's regular menu changes seasonally, but the burgers and chicken-fried offerings remain a year-round staple. Keep an eye out for specialties such as braised veal cheek or wild boar osso buco with parsnip purée, kumquat chutney and natural jus.

GREEN BEANS AND GUACAMOLE

WHITE CHOCOLATE SOUFFLÉ
with orange and grand marnier

3	TABLESPOONS UNSALTED BUTTER
3½	TABLESPOONS FLOUR
	PINCH SALT
¾	CUP MILK
4	OUNCES WHITE CHOCOLATE, GRATED
5	EGGS, SEPARATED
1	TEASPOON VANILLA EXTRACT
1	TEASPOON GRAND MARNIER
1	TEASPOON ORANGE ZEST
½	CUP SUGAR
⅔	CUP SUGAR FOR DUSTING SOUFFLÉ PAN

serves 6

Preheat oven to 375°F.

Heat butter in saucepan, whisk in flour
and salt. Gradually pour in milk, whisking,
and then bring to a boil. Remove from
heat. Add chocolate and beat in yolks,
vanilla, orange zest and Grand Marnier.
In a clean mixing bowl, whip egg whites
with sugar until frothy. Fold mixture into
batter. Butter a 6-cup soufflé dish and
sprinkle with sugar. Pour in the batter.
Bake in oven until puffed and golden.

Preheat oven to 425°F.

TO PREPARE THE FILET
Place herbs, oil, salt and pepper in a blender and purée until smooth. Set aside. Pour the herb oil over the steaks and marinate for a minimum of 2 hours. Place on a grill at high heat and sear the filet on all sides. Finish in oven to desired doneness.

TO PREPARE THE POLENTA
Bring the stock to a boil. Add the corn meal, stirring constantly. Simmer for 30 minutes and then add the remaining ingredients. Simmer an additional 5 to 8 minutes or until thick and creamy.

TO PREPARE THE DEMI GLACE
Preheat oven to 350°F. Spread bones, carrot, onion and celery on rimmed baking sheet. Roast, tossing several times, until vegetables and bones have begun to take on color, about 1 hour. Transfer roasted vegetables and bones to stockpot and add wine, water and thyme. Bring to boil. Reduce heat and simmer gently, until reduced by ¾—about 2 hours. Strain and reserve stock. Place stock and peppercorns in a pot and reduce to smooth sauce consistency. Stir in diced, cold butter before serving, 1 tablespoon butter, per cup of liquid.

TO SERVE
Ladle polenta on plates. Top with filet. Drizzle with demi glace.

FILET MIGNON
2	FILET MIGNON STEAKS
1	CUP FRESH, ASSORTED HERBS
2	TABLESPOONS OLIVE OIL
	SEA SALT AND CRACKED PEPPER

POLENTA
1	CUP CORN MEAL
3	CUPS STOCK, CHICKEN OR VEGETABLE
1	CUP ASIAGO CHEESE
4	OUNCES BUTTER
1	CUP CREAM
	HERB OIL
	SALT AND PEPPER

DEMI GLACE
3	POUNDS ASSORTED VEAL BONES
¾	POUND VEAL LEG BONE
½	CARROT, COARSELY CHOPPED
1	SMALL ONION, COARSELY CHOPPED
1	CELERY STALK, COARSELY CHOPPED
1	BOUQUET FRESH THYME
¼	CUP RED BURGUNDY WINE
8	CUPS WATER
¼	TEASPOON SALT
1	TABLESPOON WHOLE BLACK PEPPERCORNS, TOASTED
	BUTTER, COLD AND DICED

serves 2

GREEN BEANS AND GUACAMOLE

RDG + BAR ANNIE

After decades serving socialites and well-heeled clientele at the Uptown-area Café Annie, Chef Robert del Grande moved on—but he didn't have to go far. Just weeks after shuttering his flagship restaurant in 2009, the chef unveiled his renewed concept—RDG + Bar Annie— just down the Boulevard. The glossy, two-story venture reflects a more approachable atmosphere when compared to the more buttoned-up Café Annie. Just inside the door is BLVD Lounge, while Bar Annie, the grill room and an inviting patio space all unfold at the top of a dramatic staircase. With three distinct menus and a half-dozen dining areas, Chef del Grande casts a wide net that appeals to a come-as-you-are-clientele, as well as polished professionals. Within the multi-level venture, diners will find a mix of newly-developed dishes, revamped culinary creations, as well as favorites like the tortilla soup and wood-roasted rabbit enchiladas, rescued from the Café Annie era.

GREEN BEANS AND GUACAMOLE

COFFEE-ROASTED TENDERLOIN
RDG + BAR ANNIE

BEEF

2	POUNDS BEEF TENDERLOIN, TIED WITH BUTCHER'S TWINE
2	TABLESPOONS EXTRA VIRGIN OLIVE OIL
4	TABLESPOONS FINELY-GROUND COFFEE
2	TEASPOONS SALT
2	TEASPOONS BLACK PEPPER

SMOKED-CHILE ADOBO

1	OUNCE GUAJILLO CHILES, STEMS AND SEEDS REMOVED
2	CHIPOTLE CHILES, CANNED
3	TABLESPOONS EXTRA VIRGIN OLIVE OIL
1	TABLESPOON WATER
½	TEASPOON BALSAMIC VINEGAR OR RED WINE VINEGAR
1	TEASPOON FINELY-GROUND COFFEE
½	TEASPOON SALT
	PINCH BLACK PEPPER

SLOW-ROASTED ONIONS

2	LARGE YELLOW ONIONS
2	TABLESPOONS EXTRA VIRGIN OLIVE OIL
	PINCH SALT AND PEPPER
4	WOODEN SKEWERS

GARNISH

FLAT-LEAF PARSLEY SPRIGS

SALT AND PEPPER

EXTRA VIRGIN OLIVE OIL

serves 4

Preheat oven to 400°F.

TO PREPARE THE BEEF TENDERLOIN
Rub the tenderloin with the olive oil. Combine the ground coffee, salt and pepper in a small bowl and mix well. Place the tenderloin on a roasting rack, over an oven-safe pan. Roast the tenderloin for 5 minutes at 400°F, then lower the heat to 275°F and continue to roast for an additional 20 minutes or until the internal temperature of the tenderloin reaches 120°F. Remove the tenderloin from the oven and allow to rest 10 to 15 minutes before carving.

TO PREPARE THE SMOKED-CHILE ADOBO
In a dry skillet over medium heat, lightly toast the chiles until aromatic. Transfer the toasted chiles to a bowl and cover with warm water. Soak for 30 minutes to soften. On a cutting board, place the soaked chiles, skin-side down. With a knife, gently scrape off the meat from the chiles. Discard the skin. Finely mince and mash the chile meat on the cutting board to form a rough paste. Similarly, finely mince and mash the chipotle chiles on the cutting board to form a paste. In a small mixing bowl, combine the guajillo paste and the chipotle paste. Add the remaining adobo ingredients and blend well.

TO PREPARE THE SLOW-ROASTED ONIONS
Peel the onions. Cut the top and root section off the onions. Cut the onions in half through the equator to generate 4, ½-inch onion rounds. Skewer the onions with the wood skewers to hold the onion rings in place. Lightly brush with olive oil. In a hot skillet, sear the onions until browned. Drizzle some olive oil over the onions so it seeps into the onion rings. Transfer the onions to a 325°F oven. Roast the onions for 45 minutes or until the onions turn tender and buttery. Remove from the oven and drizzle with any remaining olive oil. Remove the skewers.

TO SERVE
Remove the string from the tenderloin. Carve the tenderloin into 4, thick slices. Place a slice and an onion round side-by-side on a dinner plate. Spoon some of the adobo over the meat. Garnish the onion with parsley sprigs. Sprinkle with salt and pepper and drizzle with olive oil.

GREEN BEANS AND GUACAMOLE

REEF

Staying true to his Gulf Coast roots, Chef Bryan Caswell imparts his love for fishing and the ocean in his award-winning Midtown restaurant, Reef. Diners love the spot's refined blend of locally-grown produce and use of Third-Coast-caught seafood, as do foodies on the national stage. The famed chef has twice been named a finalist for a James Beard award and even competed on the third season of The Food Network's *The Next Iron Chef*. Today, he continues to reel Reef guests in with his slow-cooked, crispy-skin snapper and roasted grouper with braised collards and pecan-shallot cracklins. Caswell's other Houston ventures include the Texas Tuscan-inspired Stella Sola, Little Bigs burger joint and the Tex-Mex outpost, El Real.

Preheat oven to 400°F.

TO PREPARE THE POMEGRANATE JUS
In a saucepan, combine pomegranate juice, verjus, shallots and peppercorns. Bring to a boil and then simmer until reduced by ¾. Remove from heat, add Thai basil and cover. Steep for 1 hour.

TO PREPARE THE PLANTAINS AND LONG BEANS
In a large pot, heat grapeseed oil and caramelize plantains and long beans. Clear a spot in the corner of the pan. Add butter and brown. Add the shallots and ginger and sweat for a few minutes. Sprinkle with sugar. Toss and sauté all ingredients. Remove from heat and drain on paper towel.

TO PREPARE THE COBIA
In a large skillet, heat olive oil over high heat. Add cobia fillets and sear on both sides until brown, about 1 minute. Remove from heat and place in oven to finish cooking, about 4 to 5 minutes.

TO SERVE
Create a bed of plantains and beans on plates. Place cobia on top and spoon pomegranate jus over fish. Garnish with pomegranate seeds and basil.

NOTE: If Cobia is unavailable, substitute with halibut or sea bass. Verjus is the juice from unripe grapes. It can be found at specialty grocery stores and online. Once opened, store verjus in the refrigerator. Long beans can be found at Asian markets. Green beans can be substituted, but do not impart the same flavor to the dish.

4	COBIA FILLETS
1	TABLESPOON OLIVE OIL

POMEGRANATE JUS

15	OUNCES POMEGRANATE JUICE, FRESH OR BOTTLED
8	OUNCES VERJUS, SEE NOTE
2	SHALLOTS, SLICED
1	TEASPOON BLACK PEPPERCORNS
1	BUNCH THAI BASIL

PLANTAINS AND LONG BEANS

4	PLANTAINS, QUARTERED LENGTHWISE AND DICED
1	BUNCH LONG BEANS
2	TABLESPOONS GRAPESEED OIL
2	TABLESPOONS BUTTER
2	SHALLOTS, MINCED
2	TABLESPOONS GINGER, MINCED
1½	TABLESPOONS RAW SUGAR

GARNISH

POMEGRANATE SEEDS

THAI BASIL, WIDE CHIFFONADE

serves 4

GREEN BEANS AND GUACAMOLE

SHRIMP SPRING ROLL
with sweet and sour sauce

SHRIMP SPRING ROLL

1   POUND SHRIMP, HEADS REMOVED, TAILS INTACT, CLEANED AND DEVEINED

1   TEASPOON FISH SAUCE

1   TEASPOON CORIANDER ROOT, CHOPPED

1   TEASPOON GARLIC, CHOPPED

½   TEASPOON WHITE PEPPER

⅔   CUP FRESH EGG NOODLES

    RICE PAPER, CUT OR SHAPED, SEE NOTE

    OIL, FOR FRYING

SWEET AND SOUR SAUCE

½   POUND FINGER CHILIES, STEMMED AND COARSELY CHOPPED

2   TABLESPOONS SUGAR

⅓   CUP WHITE VINEGAR

2   CLOVES GARLIC, CHOPPED

1   TABLESPOON FISH SAUCE

¼   CUP HONEY

1   LIME, JUICED

serves 4-6

TO PREPARE THE SAUCE
Place the chilies in a blender or food processor with the sugar, vinegar, garlic and fish sauce. Blend until minced, but not puréed. Place 1 cup of the mixture into bowl, stir in the honey and lime juice. Taste and adjust flavor.

TO PREPARE THE SPRING ROLLS
In a bowl, combine the fish sauce, coriander root, garlic and white pepper. Add the shrimp and marinate for 1 to 2 hours. Remove shrimp from bowl. Discard marinade. Wrap each shrimp in rice paper, allowing the tail to hang outside of the paper. Use the egg noodles to tie the wrap. In a heavy-bottomed pan or deep fryer, cook the shrimp rolls until golden brown. Remove and drain on plate lined with paper towels.

NOTE: Finger chilies are also known as cayenne peppers. Substitute green chilies, if fresh cayenne peppers are unavailable. Coriander root is difficult to find. Substitute with two stems of cilantro. Spring roll wrapper is cut like a house-shaped pentagon.

RISTORANTE CAVOUR

Hotel Granduca's Tuscan-inspired Ristorante Cavour—the intimate dining destination set on the ground floor of the Uptown-area boutique property—remains an under-the-radar star in the Houston area. The well-appointed space channels old-world Italy in a palette of warm earth tones and candlelight. Glass sconces, gauzy curtains and richly-upholstered Louis chairs add to the inviting charm. Under the direction of Tuscan-born Executive Chef Renato De Pirro, the signature restaurant showcases Northern Italian cuisine in an array of artfully-plated handmade pasta, seafood and meat dishes, some featuring Piedmontese beef—a particular breed of Italian cattle recognized for its tender, low-fat qualities. Save room for the crème brûlée, which arrives in a nest of crispy phyllo, topped with coconut ice cream. Note: The pool makes a serene setting for post-dinner drinks.

GREEN BEANS AND GUACAMOLE

TO PREPARE THE OSSO BUCO

Place the rosemary, sage, thyme and garlic in a piece of cheese-cloth, tie with twine and then set aside. In a flameproof casserole, heat 4 tablespoons of olive oil with the butter. Cook the minced vegetables over low heat until tender, about 15 minutes. Meanwhile, season the veal shanks with salt and pepper and lightly dust them with flour, shaking off any excess. In a heavy skillet, heat 4 tablespoons of oil and sear the veal until golden, about 5 minutes per side. When the vegetables are tender, add the veal and the herb bundle to the casserole and continue to cook, approximately 5 to 10 minutes. Remove the veal to a plate and deglaze the pan with the red wine. Place the veal back into the casserole in a single layer. Add the tomato paste and enough water to cover the meat. Cover the casserole and slowly braise over low heat until very tender—approximately 2 hours. Add water in small quantities, if necessary. Let the veal rest in the casserole.

TO PREPARE THE POLENTA

Bring water, milk and a pinch of salt to a boil in a medium saucepan. Add polenta in a slow stream, whisking vigorously until thick. Reduce heat to low and cook for approximately 30 minutes, whisking periodically. Stir in butter and Parmesan and season with salt and pepper.

TO PREPARE GREMOLATA

Stir the lemon zest, parsley and garlic together.

Serve osso buco on a bed of polenta. Spoon sauce over veal and sprinkle with gremolata. Top with herb sprigs, if desired.

OSSO BUCO

2	TABLESPOONS FLOUR, FOR DUSTING
1	SPRIG ROSEMARY
1	SPRIG SAGE
1	SPRIG THYME
2	CLOVES GARLIC
8	TABLESPOONS EXTRA VIRGIN OLIVE OIL, DIVIDED
½	STICK BUTTER
½	CUP ONION, MINCED
¼	CUP CELERY, MINCED
¼	CUP CARROTS, MINCED
4	VEAL SHANKS, 12 TO 14 OUNCES EACH
1½	CUPS RED WINE
2	TABLESPOONS TOMATO PASTE

POLENTA

½	POUND POLENTA
2	CUPS WATER
2	CUPS MILK
2	TABLESPOONS BUTTER
½	CUP PARMESAN CHEESE, GRATED
	SALT AND PEPPER

GREMOLATA

1	TABLESPOON OF LEMON ZEST, GRATED OR MINCED
1	TABLESPOON OF PARSLEY, CHOPPED
1	TEASPOON OF GARLIC, MINCED

serves 4

GREEN BEANS AND GUACAMOLE

TIRAMISU
RISTORANTE CAVOUR

8 EGG YOLKS

¾ CUP SUGAR

1 TEASPOON ESPRESSO POWDER

1 CUP MASCARPONE CHEESE

1 CUP HEAVY CREAM

2 CUPS ESPRESSO, BREWED

2 TABLESPOONS SAMBUCA, OPTIONAL,
TO BE ADDED TO THE ESPRESSO

3 DOZEN LADYFINGERS

3 TABLESPOONS COCOA POWDER,
FOR DUSTING

serves 8

In a medium bowl, beat the egg yolks with the sugar until white and fluffy. Turn off the mixer and add the espresso powder. Gently fold in the mascarpone until smooth. In a separate bowl, whisk the heavy cream until peaks form and fold it into the egg and mascarpone mixture.

Spread a spoonful of the cream mixture into the bottom of 8 cups. Pour the espresso into a shallow bowl. One by one, soak each ladyfinger in the espresso for 3 to 4 seconds and then place it in one of the cups. Top ladyfingers with a layer of the cream mixture. Repeat soaking and layering to reach the top of the cup. The last layer should be the cream mixture. Some ladyfingers may be left over. Chill the cups in the refrigerator for at least 2 hours. Dust with cocoa powder before serving.

NOTE: Pasteurized eggs are recommended. Tiramisu can also be prepared in a single glass baking dish.

SHADE

Nestled in the heart of the Heights' personality-packed 19th Street, Shade remains a neighborhood favorite, turning out eclectic, New American fare in a contemporary, olive-and-earthen-hued space. The venture, created by Chef Claire Smith and Russell Murrell in 2003, was a fast favorite in the area, thanks in part to the well-executed cuisine and smart wine list. Of course, it didn't hurt that Shade managed to circumvent the Heights' tricky dry ordinance, which bans the sale of alcohol in large parts of the community. Stop in—between shopping expeditions—for lunch, dinner and weekend brunch and enjoy hearty servings of fried shrimp and bacon grits, Gruyère macaroni and cheese and the grilled, double-cut pork chop.

Preheat oven to 325°F (convection oven) or 350°F (regular oven).

TO PREPARE THE CRUST

In a mixing bowl, using a stand or hand mixer, cream the butter and sugar. Add the egg and vanilla. Fold in the bread flour, pinch of soda and toasted hazelnuts. Refrigerate the dough for 4 hours before using. It will need to be firm to handle. Roll the dough between pieces of plastic wrap and press into either 8, 3-inch tart pans or 2, 8-inch tart pans, making sure to build the crust up the sides of the tart pans. Freeze the shells before baking. Place a piece of parchment or wax paper—big enough to cover the top— over the entire shell. Fill the shell with dried beans or pie weights to blind bake the shells, until the crust is a light golden brown around the edges—about 14 to 18 minutes in a convection oven, 20 to 25 minutes in a regular oven. Remove the pie weights and continue baking for another 7 to 10 minutes until the entire crust is light golden brown. Cool the tart shells before adding pie filling.

TO PREPARE THE FILLING

Sift the flour and sugar into a stainless steel bowl. Gradually whisk in the milk and whipping cream. Cook over a pot of boiling water, like a double boiler, constantly stirring for about 20 minutes or until thick, making sure to keep the mixture off of the sides. Whisk egg yolks in another bowl, slowly temper the yolks by gradually adding a tiny amount of the hot milk mixture to bring the temperature of the yolks to match the temperature of the milk and sugar mixture. When all of the milk has been added, put the bowl over the heat and cook for 2 minutes more. Remove the mixture from the heat and add butter and vanilla, stirring until well incorporated. Cool completely. Once the mixture is completely cooled, fold in 2 cups of the toasted and cooled coconut.

TO PREPARE THE WHIPPED-CREAM TOPPING

Chill a stainless steel mixing bowl and whisk in freezer for about 10 minutes. Whisk the heavy cream and vanilla extract until stiff peaks form.

TO ASSEMBLE

Add coconut cream filling to pie shells and top with whipped cream. Garnish with toasted coconut.

NOTE: To toast coconut, spread 2½ cups sweetened and shredded coconut on a sheet pan and bake at 350°F until light brown, about 10 to 15 minutes.

CRUST

¾	CUP PLUS 2 TABLESPOONS UNSALTED BUTTER
¾	CUP GRANULATED SUGAR
½	EGG, WHISKED
¼	TEASPOON VANILLA EXTRACT
	PINCH BAKING SODA
1¼	CUPS BREAD FLOUR
¼	POUND HAZELNUTS, TOASTED, CRUSHED AND COOLED

FILLING

¾	CUP ALL-PURPOSE FLOUR
1	CUP GRANULATED SUGAR
½	TEASPOON SALT
2⅓	CUPS 2 PERCENT MILK
1	CUP HEAVY CREAM
4	EGG YOLKS
2	TABLESPOONS BUTTER
½	TABLESPOON VANILLA EXTRACT
2	CUPS TOASTED COCONUT, COOLED, SEE NOTE

WHIPPED-CREAM TOPPING

1	QUART HEAVY CREAM
1	TEASPOON VANILLA EXTRACT

serves 8, 3-inch tarts or 2, 8-inch tarts

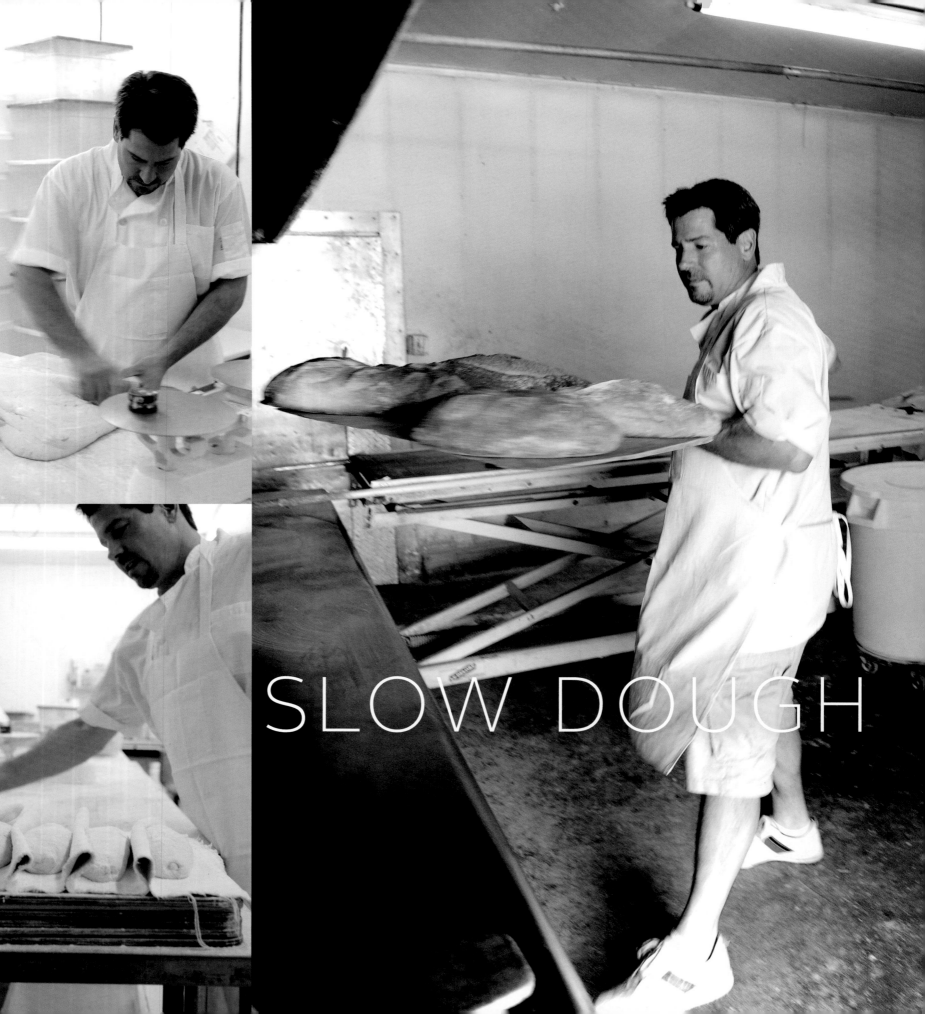

SLOW DOUGH

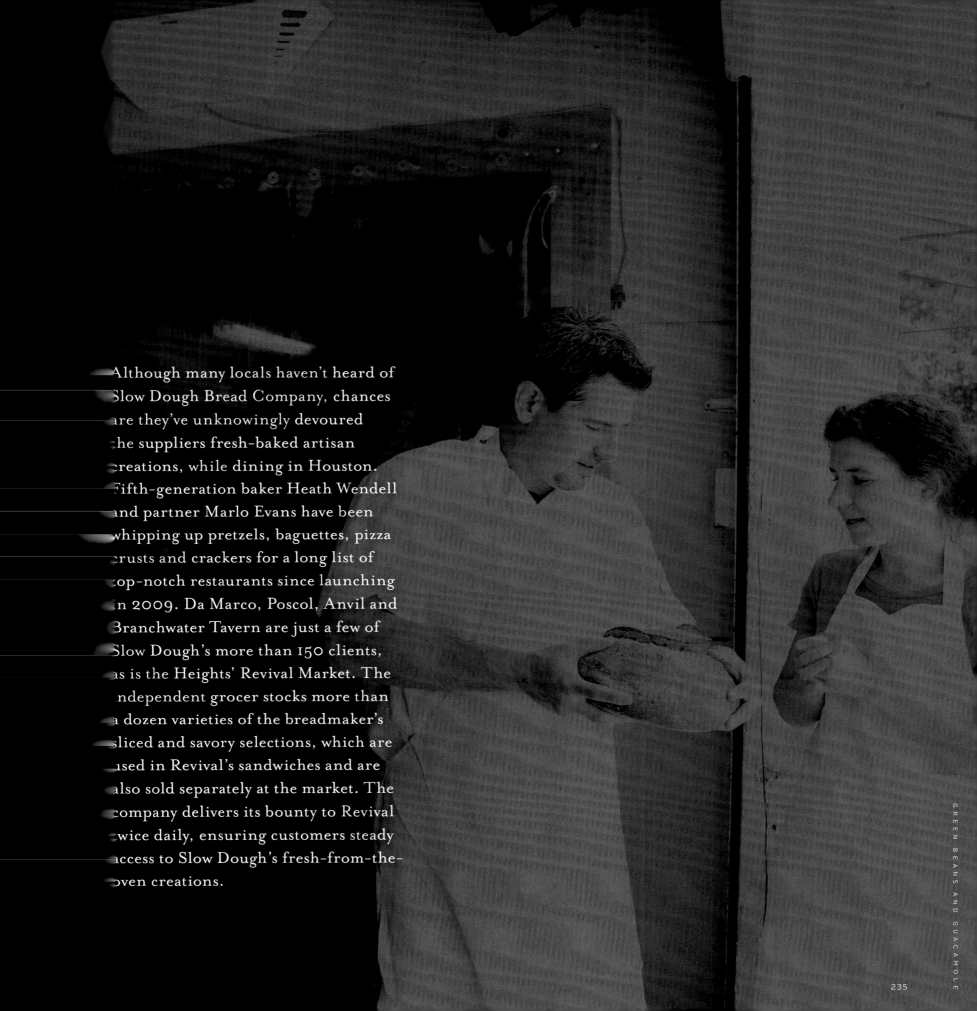

Although many locals haven't heard of
Slow Dough Bread Company, chances
are they've unknowingly devoured
the suppliers fresh-baked artisan
creations, while dining in Houston.
Fifth-generation baker Heath Wendell
and partner Marlo Evans have been
whipping up pretzels, baguettes, pizza
crusts and crackers for a long list of
top-notch restaurants since launching
in 2009. Da Marco, Poscol, Anvil and
Branchwater Tavern are just a few of
Slow Dough's more than 150 clients,
as is the Heights' Revival Market. The
independent grocer stocks more than
a dozen varieties of the breadmaker's
sliced and savory selections, which are
used in Revival's sandwiches and are
also sold separately at the market. The
company delivers its bounty to Revival
twice daily, ensuring customers steady
access to Slow Dough's fresh-from-the-
oven creations.

SEMOLINA BREAD
SLOW DOUGH

1½	CUPS COLD WATER
1	TEASPOON INSTANT DRY YEAST
3¼	CUPS DURUM FLOUR
1	TABLESPOON SUGAR
¼	CUP EXTRA VIRGIN OLIVE OIL
1½	TEASPOON SEA SALT

makes 2 loaves

Pour water into mixing bowl. Add flour. Using a dough hook, mix on low speed until fully incorporated. Let stand for 20 minutes. This is called an "autolyse"— it allows the water to absorb into the flour gently versus being mixed in. Add the olive oil and sugar. Mix for 20 seconds on low speed and then on medium speed for 2 minutes. Add yeast. Mix for 1 minute on medium speed, then add the sea salt. Mix on medium speed until dough looks smooth.

Find a resting bowl with enough space for the dough to double in size. Coat bowl lightly in olive oil. Put dough into resting bowl and cover bowl with a damp cloth. Let dough rise for 2 hours at ambient temperature.

Lightly dust countertop with flour. Remove dough from bowl and divide into 2 equal pieces. Using both hands, shape each piece of dough into a round ball. Place each loaf, seam side down, on a flour-dusted plate. Cover each plate loosely with plastic wrap and place in refrigerator for 2½ hours. Remove from refrigerator and place on countertop. Let rest until dough reaches ambient temperature.

Preheat oven to 375°F. Place a pizza stone in the oven. Using a spray bottle, spray the dough with water and sprinkle with sesame seeds. Using a very sharp knife, make a cut in each loaf as a single line across the top. Slide each loaf off of plate and onto pizza stone. Bake for 30 to 35 minutes or until golden. Remove loaves from oven and place on cooling rack. Let cool completely before slicing.

TO PREPARE THE BIGA

In a small bowl, dissolve active dry yeast in warm water. Transfer to a mixing bowl and add the room-temperature water. Add flour and mix until it becomes pancake batter-like consistency. Remove from the bowl and place in a large bowl. Let rest for 2 hours at ambient temperature. Place in refrigerator for 12 hours.

TO PREPARE THE CIABATTA

Pour water into mixing bowl. Add flour and mix on low speed using the dough hook until fully incorporated. Let stand for 20 minutes. This is called an "autolyse"— it allows the water to absorb into the flour gently versus being mixed in. Dissolve yeast in warm milk and add to the mixing bowl. Also add the olive oil and biga. Mix on low speed for 30 seconds. Mix on medium for 2 minutes and then add sea salt. Continue mixing until dough "comes together" and pulls off the mixing bowl and has a smooth texture. Remove the dough. Let rise at ambient temperature for 3 hours, folding dough each hour, end over end.

Lightly dust countertop with flour and place dough on counter. Lightly tap the dough out with your hands to flatten it to a thickness of 1½-inches.

Cut dough into 4-inch by 8-inch rectangles. Cover a sheet pan with a kitchen towel and thoroughly dust with flour. Transfer rectangles of dough onto kitchen towel. Let rise for 1 to 1½ hours.

Preheat oven to 385°F and insert a pizza stone. When dough becomes airy, roll it gently off the towel and onto the stone, so the floured side is up. Mist the oven walls with water using a spray bottle to create steam. Bake for 25 to 35 minutes or until golden. Remove from oven. Let cool for 20 minutes on a cooling rack. Slice and serve.

NOTE: Biga is a starter used in Italian bread recipes.

BIGA	
⅛	TEASPOON ACTIVE DRY YEAST
2	TABLESPOONS WARM WATER, 105°F TO 115°F
⅓	CUP ROOM-TEMPERATURE WATER
1	CUP BREAD FLOUR

CIABATTA	
½	TEASPOON ACTIVE DRY YEAST
2	TABLESPOONS WARM MILK, 105°F TO 115°F
⅔	CUP ROOM-TEMPERATURE WATER
1	TABLESPOON OLIVE OIL
2	CUPS BREAD FLOUR
1¾	TEASPOON SEA SALT

makes 2 loaves

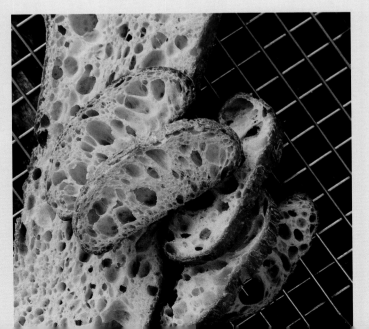

SORREL
URBAN BISTRO

The farm-to-table focus of Sorrel Urban Bistro is nothing new for restaurateur Ray Salti and Chef Soren Pedersen. The duo—who are also responsible for Ray's Gourmet Country in Fulshear—bring their shared commitment to delivering certified natural meats and sustainable seafood dishes to the Upper Kirby area. The 4,000-square-foot space is light and airy, marked by maple finishes, floor-to-ceiling windows and a dual French kitchen that live-streams video of Chef Pederson at work on dining room monitors. Near the entrance, a 30-seat charcuterie bar offers sliced-to-order meats and artisan cheeses. On Sorrel's menu, guests will find a culinary line-up that changes several times a week touting everything from seared Muscovy duck and grilled veal mignon to Colorado rack of lamb and Wagyu beef risotto.

GREEN BEANS AND GUACAMOLE

PEAR MARZIPAN
SORREL

STREUSEL

1	CUP FLOUR
1	CUP BROWN SUGAR
1	CUP SUGAR
1	TABLESPOON CINNAMON
1	TABLESPOON VANILLA
½	POUND MARZIPAN

PEARS

6	PEARS, CORED AND SLICED
¼	POUND BUTTER, SLICED

CRUST

9	CUPS FLOUR
1	CUP SUGAR
1	POUND BUTTER
5	EGGS

makes 2, 11-inch by 11-inch tart rounds

Preheat oven to 375°F.

TO PREPARE THE CRUST
In a large bowl, combine the sugar and butter and mix until smooth. Stir in the flour and eggs until dough forms and pulls away from the edges of the bowl. Chill in the refrigerator for 30 minutes. Remove and turn dough out onto a work surface. Divide the dough into 2 portions. Roll out the dough and press into tart pans. Prick the tart shells with a fork, cover with foil and pie weights. Bake for 15 minutes or until edges are golden. Remove the foil and the weights and bake another 15 minutes. Remove from the oven and cool completely.

TO PREPARE THE STREUSEL
Combine all ingredients in a bowl. Mix well.

TO PREPARE THE TARTS
Place a thin layer of streusel onto the crust. Fan the sliced pears over the filling. Dot the pears with butter. Spread another layer of the streusel over the tart. Bake at 350°F for approximately 1 hour or until golden. Let the tarts cool to room temperature before serving.

Preheat oven to 425°F.

TO PREPARE THE LAMB
Place herbs, oil, salt and pepper in a blender and purée until smooth. Place the rack of lamb in a roasting pan and pour the herb oil all over. Marinate for a minimum of 2 hours. Heat a grill to high heat and sear the lamb on all sides. Finish in the oven until desired doneness.

TO PREPARE THE POTATO
Preheat oven to 350°F. Toss the potato wedges with oil and season with salt and pepper. Roast in a baking pan until tender and golden.

TO PREPARE THE DEMI GLACE
Preheat oven to 350°F. Spread bones, carrot, onion and celery on rimmed baking sheet. Roast, tossing several times, until vegetables and bones have begun to take on color, about 1 hour. Transfer roasted vegetables and bones to stockpot. Add wine, water and thyme and bring to boil. Reduce heat and simmer gently until reduced by ¾—about 2 hours. Strain and reserve stock. Place stock and currants in a pot and reduce to smooth sauce consistency. Stir in diced, cold butter before serving, one tablespoon butter, per cup of liquid.

NOTE: Purchased demi glace can be substituted.

RACK OF LAMB

1	RACK OF LAMB
1	CUP FRESH ASSORTED HERBS
2	TABLESPOONS OLIVE OIL
	SEA SALT AND CRACKED PEPPER

ROASTED POTATO

1	YUKON GOLD POTATO, CUT INTO WEDGES
	OLIVE OIL, TO TASTE
	SEA SALT, TO TASTE
	FRESH GROUND PEPPER

DEMI GLACE

3	POUNDS ASSORTED VEAL BONES
¾	POUND VEAL LEG BONE
½	CARROT, COARSELY CHOPPED
1	SMALL ONION, COARSELY CHOPPED
1	CELERY STALK, COARSELY CHOPPED
1	BOUQUET FRESH THYME
8	CUPS WATER
¼	CUP RED BURGUNDY WINE
¼	TEASPOON SALT
3	TABLESPOONS RED CURRANTS
	BUTTER, COLD AND DICED

serves 4

SORRENTO RISTORANTE

Lower Westheimer's restaurant row shines with the 2003 addition of the classically-upscale Sorrento Ristorante. Owner Abbas Hussein and his staff transport guests to southern Italy inside an elegant old-world-inspired interior. Painted murals, high ceilings and linen-topped tables adorn the multi-room dining space. Near the entrance, a small bar features a mural of the Amalfi coast and makes room for a piano, which provides romantics with a live dinner-time soundtrack, several nights a week. Since opening, Sorrento has earned a loyal following—thanks to its friendly service and linger-worthy cuisine—so much so that the restaurant expanded with a second Kingwood location in 2011. Perfectly-sauced, house-made pastas earn rave reviews, as does the goat cheese-stuffed rack of lamb and braised short ribs. Don't miss the deliciously-filling Sunday brunch.

WILD-MUSHROOM RISOTTO
with sage, white truffle oil and black truffle shaving

6 CUPS CHICKEN BROTH, DIVIDED

3 TABLESPOONS OLIVE OIL, DIVIDED

2 POUNDS WILD MUSHROOMS, THINLY SLICED, CHANTERELLES, SHITAKES, MORELS, HEN OF WOODS

2 SHALLOTS, DICED

1½ CUPS ARBORIO RICE

½ CUP DRY WHITE WINE

SEA SALT

FRESHLY GROUND BLACK PEPPER

3 FRESH SAGE LEAVES

⅓ CUP PARMESAN CHEESE, GRATED

4 TABLESPOONS WHITE TRUFFLE OIL, OPTIONAL

1 WHOLE BLACK TRUFFLE, OPTIONAL

serves 6–8

In a saucepan, warm the broth over low heat. In a large saucepan, warm 2 tablespoons olive oil over medium-high heat. Stir in the wild mushrooms, sage, sea salt and 2 tablespoons of truffle oil and cook until soft, about 3 minutes. Remove mushrooms and their liquid, set aside. Add 1 tablespoon olive oil to skillet and stir in the shallots. Cook 1 minute. Add rice, stirring to coat with oil, about 2 minutes. When the rice has taken on a pale, golden color, pour in wine, stirring constantly until the wine is fully absorbed. Add ½-cup broth to the rice and stir until the broth is absorbed. Continue adding broth ½ cup at a time, stirring continuously, until the liquid is absorbed and the rice is al dente—about 15 to 20 minutes. Remove from heat and stir in mushrooms with their liquid, butter, remaining 2 tablespoons of truffle oil and Parmesan. Season with salt and pepper. Shave a few thin slices of black truffle and serve.

2 SKINLESS, BONELESS CHICKEN BREASTS, BUTTERFLIED AND THEN CUT IN HALF

SALT AND FRESHLY-GROUND BLACK PEPPER

ALL-PURPOSE FLOUR, FOR DREDGING

6 TABLESPOONS UNSALTED BUTTER

6 TABLESPOONS EXTRA VIRGIN OLIVE OIL

⅓ CUP FRESH LEMON JUICE

½ CUP CHICKEN STOCK

¼ CUP BRINED CAPERS, RINSED

4 THINLY-SLICED FRESH LEMON ROUNDS

½ POUND MIXED, SLICED MUSHROOMS, OPTIONAL

serves 2

Place chicken between 2 sheets of plastic wrap, lightly pound chicken. Season chicken with salt and pepper. Dredge chicken in flour and shake off excess. In a large skillet over medium-high heat, melt 2 tablespoons of butter with 6 tablespoons olive oil. When butter and oil start to sizzle, add all 4 pieces of chicken and cook until lightly browned, flip and cook other side for 3 minutes. Remove the chicken from the pan and drain off the butter and oil. Place the chicken back into the pan on medium-high heat. Add capers, sliced mushrooms and lemon rounds. Wait 1 minute and then add the wine to the pan. Wait another minute and then add lemon juice and chicken stock. Finally, add the remaining 4 tablespoons of butter to the pan, lower the heat to low. Once the butter is melted into a sauce consistency, turn the heat off and serve.

GREEN BEANS AND GUACAMOLE

T'AFIA

Dubbed the "Alice Waters of the Third Coast," German-born, Houston-reared chef Monica Pope has been revolutionizing Houston's culinary scene since she opened her first restaurant in 1992—experience that earned her a James Beard nomination and a spot on Bravo's *Top Chef Masters*. Today, she shares her passion for connecting local farmers and consumers in her successful Midtown Farmers Market, weekly cooking classes and t'afia restaurant. In the latter, Chef Pope draws heavily on regional products that fill her always-evolving menu. Diners might find grilled rabbit meatballs and smoked trout ravioli offered during one visit and Kobe bulgogi and mascarpone-lemon panna cotta served up another day. Stop in for happy hour, Tuesday through Thursday, when Chef Pope offers complimentary Lounge Menu bites with the purchase of an alcoholic beverage.

CHICKPEA FRIES
with red curry sambal ketchup

T'AFIA

CHICKPEA FRIES

2½	CUPS CHICKPEA FLOUR
1	TEASPOON KOSHER SALT
	BLACK PEPPER
	TURMERIC
	CUMIN
4	CUPS WATER, BRING TO A BOIL
½	CUPS FLOUR, FOR DUSTING
	OIL, FOR FRYING

RED CURRY SAMBAL KETCHUP

3	TABLESPOONS CORIANDER SEEDS
3	BUNCHES CILANTRO
4	CHOPPED SHALLOTS
3	CLOVES GARLIC, CHOPPED
6	RED FRESNO CHILES, SEEDED AND CHOPPED
4	KAFFIR LIME LEAVES
½	TEASPOON GROUND PEPPER
1	TABLESPOON GROUND NUTMEG
3	CUPS GRAPESEED OR POMACE OLIVE OIL, NOT EXTRA VIRGIN
2	TABLESPOONS GRATED FRESH GINGER
3	TABLESPOONS LEMON JUICE
	SALT
	SAMBAL, AS NEEDED
	KETCHUP, AS NEEDED

serves 4

TO PREPARE THE FRIES
Bring water to a boil and add the chickpea flour and spices to taste. Cook for 10 minutes. Pour onto oiled sheet pan and chill. Cut into 3-inch-long French fries. Dust with flour and fry for 4 minutes.

TO PREPARE THE KETCHUP
Toast the coriander seeds, let cool and then grind in spice grinder. Combine with all other ingredients and process. Mix equal parts red curry paste and ketchup together in small bowl. Add Sambal to desired heat and spiciness.

CHORIZO DATES WRAPPED IN BACON
with chermoula  TAFIA

CHORIZO DATES

12	DATES, PITTED AND CUT IN HALF, PREFERABLY MEDJOOL
1	MEDIUM CHORIZO SAUSAGE, CASING REMOVED
24	SLICES BACON, SLICED IN HALF

CHERMOULA

½	TABLESPOON GARLIC CLOVES, CHOPPED
½	BUNCH CILANTRO, FINELY CHOPPED
½	BUNCH PARSLEY, FINELY CHOPPED
½	CUP PAPRIKA
1	TABLESPOON CUMIN SEED, TOASTED AND GROUND
½	TABLESPOON CAYENNE
1½	TABLESPOONS SALT
¼	TABLESPOON PEPPER
¼	CUP LIME JUICE
½	CUP OLIVE OIL

serves 6

Preheat oven to 350°F.

TO PREPARE THE CHERMOULA
Mix all ingredients in a bowl.

TO PREPARE THE DATES
Overstuff each date half with chorizo. Wrap in bacon and place together in a pan. Bake for 7 minutes or until crispy around edges.

TO SERVE
Swizzle dates with chermoula and serve.

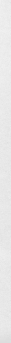

GREEN BEANS AND GUACAMOLE

THE GROVE

Nestled in Downtown's 12-acre Discovery Green park, The Grove restaurant brings rustic American cuisine to the heart of the city in an ultra-urban, 10,000-square-foot space. Created by the Schiller Del Grande Restaurant Group—the masterminds behind RDG + Bar Annie and Ava Kitchen & Whiskey Bar—The Grove opened in 2008, quickly winning the hearts of Houston's well-dressed. Beyond the brick-and-glass façade, warm wood tones, soaring ceilings and sleek olive-green banquettes add to the interior's allure, complimented by exposed brick accents and a series of Poul Henningsen-designed artichoke pendant lamps. On the well-edited menu, items like the grilled skirt steak and gourmet burgers shine, aided in part by the restaurant's on-site herb and tomato garden. On breezy Houston nights, venture upstairs to the open-air patio space for specialty cocktails and spectacular views of the Downtown skyline.

GREEN BEANS AND GUACAMOLE

259

SHRIMP MEATBALLS
with rémoulade sauce

SHRIMP MEATBALLS

2 POUNDS GULF SHRIMP

2 TABLESPOONS BUTTER

2 GARLIC CLOVES, MINCED

½ WHITE ONION, MINCED

1 SERRANO PEPPER, SEEDED AND MINCED

2 OUNCES MEXICAN CHORIZO

1 EGG, LIGHTLY BEATEN

2 TABLESPOONS HEAVY CREAM

½ TEASPOON SALT

WOODEN SKEWERS OR TOOTHPICKS

RÉMOULADE

½ CUP KETCHUP

½ CUP MAYONNAISE

2 TABLESPOONS EXTRA VIRGIN OLIVE OIL

1 TABLESPOON LIME JUICE

1 TABLESPOON WHITE ONION, MINCED

1 SERRANO PEPPER, FINELY MINCED

1 TEASPOON FRESH TARRAGON LEAVES, MINCED

PINCH SALT AND PEPPER

serves 8–10 appetizers

TO PREPARE THE RÉMOULADE
Combine all of the ingredients in a bowl and mix well. Set aside.

TO PREPARE THE MEATBALLS
Peel and devein the shrimp. Pass the shrimp through a meat grinder. Alternatively, place the shrimp in a food processor and pulse to finely chop. Transfer the shrimp to a mixing bowl. In a skillet, heat 1 tablespoon of butter over medium heat. Add the minced garlic, onion and serrano pepper and sauté briefly. Transfer to the bowl with the shrimp. In the same skillet, sauté the ground chorizo until fully cooked. Pour off any fat and then transfer the chorizo to the bowl with the shrimp and mix well. Then add the beaten egg, heavy cream and salt and mix well. Heat a pot of lightly-salted water to a simmer. With a small ice cream scoop or a small spoon, form small meatballs and gently drop them into the simmering water, about 10 at a time, for 2 to 4 minutes or until cooked through. Remove from the water and cool.

TO SERVE
Heat the remaining 1 tablespoon of butter in a skillet. Add the meatballs and sauté until lightly brown and heated through. Skewer each meatball and serve with rémoulade.

TONY'S

Society heavyweights, date night duos and business clientele fill Tony Vallone's iconic Italian namesake nightly. Houston's culinary frontrunner is known for delivering some of the best service and world-class cuisine in the city. Inside the restaurant, an eye-catching water wall welcomes guests into the contemporary space, which is adorned in cinnamon-hued accents, skylights and a glassed kitchen. Artwork by Robert Rauschenberg and Donald Sultan hang high above the dining room, while Jesus Moroles' custom, 12-foot "Three Graces" sculpture soars in the center. Tony's European-style menu mixes creative appetizers, pastas, steaks and a variety of fish, prepared by fresh-faced Chef Grant Gordon. Don't leave before digging into the sky-high soufflé for dessert.

Preheat oven to 350°F.

TO PREPARE THE SAUCE

Spread the walnuts evenly on a sheet tray and toast in the oven for approximately 3 to 5 minutes or until walnuts are brown. Add the walnuts, red onions, garlic, sugar, vinegar and lemon juice to a food processor. Begin to chop. While the ingredients are being pulverized, slowly drizzle in the olive oil. After the olive oil is incorporated, finish with the parsley.

TO PREPARE THE GARLIC CHIPS

Shave the garlic as thin as possible, either on a mandolin or truffle slicer. Add them to a pot with the cold milk. Bring to a boil and remove from the heat. Strain the garlic and pat it dry. Fry the garlic until crispy and season with salt and pepper.

TO SERVE

Spread agresto sauce on plate. Place salmon on serving dish. Top with garlic chips and garnish with walnuts, parsley and more sauce, if needed.

SALMON

3	PIECES SALMON, 1½ OUNCES EACH
3	TABLESPOONS AGRESTO SAUCE, SEE RECIPE
12	GARLIC CHIPS
5	WALNUTS, TOASTED, FOR GARNISH

AGRESTO SAUCE

4	CUPS WALNUTS, TOASTED
1	CUP RED ONIONS, CHOPPED
5	GARLIC CLOVES
¼	CUP SUGAR
2	CUPS EXTRA VIRGIN OLIVE OIL
1	CUP WHITE WINE VINEGAR
1	LEMON, JUICED
2	TABLESPOONS ITALIAN PARSLEY, CHOPPED

GARLIC CHIPS

10	GARLIC CLOVES, SHAVED THIN
2	CUPS MILK
	SALT AND PEPPER
	OIL FOR FRYING

serves 2

GREEN BEANS AND GUACAMOLE

DUCK RIGATONI
with Taleggio sauce

TONY'S

4   LARGE RIGATONI, COOKED AL DENTE

3   TABLESPOONS DUCK CONFIT MIX

¼   CUP TALEGGIO SAUCE

⅓   CUP DEMI GLAZE

1   TEASPOON PARSLEY, CHOPPED

DUCK CONFIT MIX

1   CUP DUCK CONFIT MIX, SHREDDED

⅓   CUP PARMESAN CHEESE, GRATED

⅓   CUP DEMI GLAZE

1   TABLESPOONS BALSAMIC VINEGAR

    SALT AND PEPPER

TALEGGIO SAUCE

5   TABLESPOONS BUTTER

4   TABLESPOONS ALL-PURPOSE FLOUR

4   CUPS MILK

2   CUPS TALEGGIO CHEESE, RIND REMOVED

    SALT AND PEPPER

serves 1

TO PREPARE THE DUCK CONFIT MIX
Pull the duck confit from the bone and shred it apart with your hands. In a mixing bowl, combine the duck, Parmesan, demi glaze, balsamic, salt and pepper until evenly incorporated. Set aside to cool. Once cool, put the mix into a piping bag with a hole small enough to fit into the rigatoni and stuff.

TO PREPARE THE SAUCE
Melt the butter in a pot. Add the flour and stir until it turns a nice blonde color. Add the milk, continuously stirring. Bring to a boil and then turn the heat to low. Whisk in the Taleggio. Remove from heat. Season with salt and pepper.

TO SERVE
Spread a small amount of the duck confit mix on a plate. Drizzle with demi glaze. Place stuffed rigatoni on top. Top with Taleggio sauce and garnish with parsley.

NOTE: Demi glaze and duck confit mix can be found at gourmet and specialty markets.

TONY MANDOLA'S

After decades operating their iconic Gulf Coast seafood business in strip-center settings, restaurateur power couple Tony and Phyllis Mandola upgraded in 2011, moving to a dramatic, stand-alone location in Houston's Montrose neighborhood. It's been a long time coming for the duo, who both grew up in the food service industry, with Tony launching his career at Ninfa's on Navigation and marrying Ninfa Laurenzo's daughter, Phyllis, in the process. At the pair's new, French Quarter-inspired namesake, wrought-iron accents, flickering gas-lamp lighting and a stunning fountain serve as a welcome to guests. Inside, the 6,700-square-foot restaurant is significantly larger than the previous River Oaks outpost, making room for an expanded kitchen and coal-fired oven. Dig into crispy, new pizzas like Mama's Gumbo with a dark roux crabmeat, mozzarella and Parmesan, along with a slice of Tony Mandola's famous key-lime custard.

SHRIMP COCKTAIL VINCENTE'S

18	MEDIUM SHRIMP, BOILED, PEELED AND DEVEINED
3	OUNCES COCKTAIL SAUCE
½	CUP PICO DE GALLO
½	AVOCADO, PEELED, SEEDED AND CHOPPED
	TORTILLA CHIPS, FOR SERVING

serves 4 (appetizer)

Combine shrimp, cocktail sauce, pico de gallo and avocado in a mixing bowl. Transfer mixture to a bowl and serve with a side of tortilla chips.

NOTE: For cocktail sauce recipe, see appendix.

½	POUND RED KIDNEY BEANS, RINSED AND PICKED OVER
¼	GALLON OF WATER
8	OUNCES WHOLE TOMATOES, PEELED AND HAND-CRUSHED
⅓	POUND YELLOW ONIONS, CHOPPED
¼	POUND CELERY, CHOPPED
⅓	POUND GREEN BELL PEPPER, CHOPPED
1¼	OUNCES CHICKEN BASE, SEE NOTE
1	TEASPOON CUMIN, GROUND
½	TEASPOON BLACK PEPPER, GROUND
1	TEASPOON CAYENNE PEPPER
½	OUNCE GARLIC, CHOPPED
12	OUNCES WHITE RICE, COOKED

serves 4

Place beans and water in a pot and bring to a boil. Once water is boiling, add the tomatoes and boil for 45 minutes. In a separate pot, sauté onions, celery and green bell peppers over medium heat for about 2 minutes. Add chicken base, cumin, black pepper, cayenne and garlic to the sautéed vegetables and cook for about 3 minutes. Add vegetable mixture to red beans and tomatoes. Stir well and cook until they are soft. Serve over 3 ounces of cooked white rice.

NOTE: Chicken base differs from bouillon or stock and comes in a jar. One cup of additional water may be needed for proper consistency. If desired, sausage can be added to the recipe.

ZELKO BISTRO

GREEN BEANS AND GUACAMOLE

Heights' residents can thank Chef Jamie Zelko for bringing New American comfort food to the neighborhood at her rustic-chic Zelko Bistro. Set inside a 1920s bungalow, the 46-seat space is warmly-inviting, marked by wooden floors, butcher-block tables, antique Ball jar pendant lights and a shiplap ceiling. Chef Zelko—an alumna of Jean-George's Bank, Brennan's and Ibiza—takes a diner-inspired approach to her locally-sourced cuisine. Find playful dishes like the Captain Crunch-breaded fried pickles, the St. Arnolds-braised short ribs and powdered-sugar-dusted funnel cake—just like at the carnival. Look for Mama Zelko's house-made preserves—in flavors like peach & thyme, jalapeño and pickled-watermelon rind—which are available to-go.

TO PREPARE THE THREE-GRAIN MIX

Cook all grains separately. For the quinoa, bring 1 quart of water to a boil in a large saucepan. Add the quinoa, stir once and return to a boil. Cook uncovered over medium heat for 12 minutes. Strain and rinse well with cold water, shaking the sieve well to remove all moisture. For the couscous, bring 1 quart of water to a boil in a large saucepan. Add 1 teaspoon harissa paste to the water. Place the dry couscous in a shallow bowl or a small pan. Remove water once it boils and pour over dried couscous, cover pan with plastic wrap and let sit for at least 5 minutes. Remove plastic and gently fluff with a fork.

FOR THE WHOLE GRAIN BARLEY

Soaking barley in water overnight can reduce cooking time. Use 2 cups of water for each cup of barley for the soak. Rinse barley first using a strainer. Pick out any debris that might have made it through processing. Use 2½ to 3 cups water to 1 cup barley. Add the water to a pot and bring to a boil. Bring water to a boil. Add barley to boiling water and stir together. Cover the pot with a lid and reduce to low heat. If barley was presoaked overnight, cook for 15 minutes. Otherwise, cook barley for 35 to 40 minutes. When al dente, cool down on a sheet pan lined with parchment paper.

FOR THE INFUSED HERB OIL

Bring a large pot of water to a boil with salt. Blanch the basil leaves for 1 minute in boiling water. Using a strainer, remove leaves from water, drain well and squeeze out as much excess liquid as possible. Place the basil leaves in a food processor or blender with ½ cup oil and blend until smooth. Remove the purée and store in a glass container. Refrigerate for at least 1 day to intensify the color. When ready to use, strain oil through a fine mesh strainer. For ease of use in garnishing dishes, put into a small, plastic squeeze bottle.

TO SERVE

When all 3 grains are cool and dry, transfer them to a large bowl. Add the cucumbers, onion, tomato, parsley, mint, olive oil, vinegar, lemon juice, lime juice, garlic, salt and pepper. Toss well. Add bunch of baby arugula and mix. Serve on plates and drizzle with herb oil. Top with grated Parmesan.

NOTE: Zelko uses the Texas grains from Homestead Gristmill. Harissa is a Middle Eastern chili paste and can be found at most grocery stores. The herb oil can be stored for up to 1 week and can also be frozen.

THREE-GRAIN MIX

3	QUARTS WATER
1½	CUPS QUINOA, RINSED
1	CUP WHOLE GRAIN BARLEY, DRY
1	CUP COUSCOUS, DRY
2	CUCUMBERS, PEELED, ENDS TRIMMED, DICED SMALL
1	RED ONION, DICED SMALL
2	LARGE TOMATOES, SEEDED, DICED SMALL
2	CLOVES GARLIC, MINCED
1	BUNCH ITALIAN PARSLEY LEAVES, CHOPPED
1	BUNCH MINT LEAVES, CHOPPED
½	CUP EXTRA VIRGIN OLIVE OIL
½	CUP RED WINE VINEGAR
1	LEMON, JUICED
1	LIME, JUICED
2	TEASPOONS SALT
1	TEASPOON FRESHLY GROUND BLACK PEPPER
1	TEASPOON HARISSA PASTE, SEE NOTE
	BUNCH OF BABY ARUGULA
	PARMESAN, GRATED

INFUSED HERB OIL

3	CUPS PACKED, FRESH ORGANIC BASIL LEAVES
¼	TEASPOON KOSHER OR SEA SALT
½	CUP EXTRA VIRGIN OLIVE OIL OR GRAPESEED OIL

serves 6–8

TEXAS BROWN BAY SHRIMP & GRITS

ZELKO BISTRO

SWEET SOY AGAVE NECTAR

1½	CUPS SOY SAUCE
1½	CUPS AGAVE NECTAR, DARK
1½	CUPS SWEET GARLIC CHILI SAUCE, SEE RECIPE

SWEET CHILI SAUCE

½	CUP GRANULATED SUGAR
½	CUP WATER
½	TEASPOON KOSHER SALT
5	RED FINGER CHILIES, COARSELY CHOPPED
⅛	CUP RICE WINE VINEGAR
⅛	CUP WHITE VINEGAR
1	TABLESPOONS GARLIC, COARSELY CHOPPED
1	PINCH XANTHAN GUM
1½	TABLESPOONS OLIVE OIL

GARNISH

½	POUND APPLE-SMOKED BACON, COOKED UNTIL CRISP AND CHOPPED
	BUNCH SCALLIONS, SLICED THIN

serves 10

TO PREPARE THE SWEET CHILI SAUCE

In a saucepot, heat olive oil and sweat garlic and finger chilies until soft. Add rice wine vinegar and white vinegar. When deglazed, add sugar, water and xanthan gum to thicken. Bring to a simmer, season with salt and remove from heat. When it coats the back of a spoon, place hot liquid in a shallow steel pan and chill.

TO PREPARE THE SWEET SOY AGAVE NECTAR

Combine chili sauce, soy sauce and agave nectar in a bowl and whisk until fully emulsified. Pour into squeeze bottles.

TO PREPARE THE POLENTA GRITS

In a large, heavy saucepan, combine 1¼ quarts of water with the 5 quarts of chicken stock. Bring to a boil and slowly add the polenta, whisking constantly. Reduce the heat to low and simmer, stirring often with a large wooden spoon, until the polenta thickens, about 25 minutes. Add the butter and bacon fat and stir until melted. Add the white cheddar and stir well. Adjust seasoning to taste

TO PREPARE THE SHRIMP

In a large bowl, toss the shrimp with the dry spices and olive oil. In a sauté pan, add olive oil and cook the garlic and shallots over medium heat until translucent. Add the shrimp and cook for 1 to 2 minutes.

TO SERVE

Spoon warm grits into a deep bowl, add 4 shrimp and top with crisp bacon. Finish with scallions and sweet agave nectar.

NOTE: Honey can be substituted for agave nectar. Brazos Valley White Cheddar can be found at gourmet and culinary markets.

WHITE GRISTMILL POLENTA

1¼	QUARTS HOMESTEAD GRISTMILL STONE GROUND POLENTA
1	CUPS BRAZOS VALLEY WHITE CHEDDAR OR STORE-BOUGHT WHITE CHEDDAR
2½	CUPS CHICKEN STOCK
2½	CUPS WATER
8	OUNCES UNSALTED BUTTER, CUBED
4	OUNCES BACON FAT
	SALT AND FRESHLY CRACKED BLACK PEPPER

SHRIMP

1	TEASPOONS PAPRIKA
1	TEASPOONS CAYENNE PEPPER
1	TEASPOONS BLACK PEPPER
1	TEASPOONS CELERY SEED
1	TEASPOONS SALT
40	BROWN BAY SHRIMP, CLEANED AND DEVEINED
¼	CUP MINCED GARLIC
¼	CUP MINCED SHALLOTS
	OLIVE OIL, TO COAT SHRIMP AND TO SAUTÉ

GREEN BEANS

and

GUACAMOLE

A COLLECTION OF FAVORITE RECIPES *from Houston's Top Restaurants & Their Chefs*

STEERING COMMITTEE

HEATH BARNES
GARY BECKER
JOANNE BOWMAN
KRISTI BREAUX
BART BROWN
KAY BROWN
CANDACE BURNS
JAN COBDEN
PAM DEZEVALLOS
SHELLY DEZEVALLOS
GAIL DONAHUE
LYNN EINKAUF
MARY FLORES
BOB FUMAGALLI
MARIA GLYMPH
IVONNE HALLARD
BELINDA HILLHOUSE
CORKY HILLHOUSE
SUSAN KROHN
SANDY LAFORGE
LADEANNE LARSON
CAROL LIPWORTH
JIM LYKES
LAURIE MCNAY
LISA MIRANDA
KATHY MITCHELL
KERRI MORRISON
MATTHEW PACETTI
RICH PANCIOLI
STEPHANIE PANCIOLI
KAREN PENNER
CYNTHIA PIRO
RON PUNNEO
REBECCA RAY
BRENDA RUTT
JON SHAFFER
AMY SKODA
STEPHEN SKODA
KAREN STALL
DONNA VALLONE
BETH WALKER
RAYMOND WALKER
VICKI WEYEL

COOKING & TESTING COMMITTEE

SUNNY ALLGAIER
HEATH BARNES
KEN BREAUX
KRISTI BREAUX
BART BROWN
KAY BROWN
CANDACE BURNS
JAN COBDEN
PAM DEZEVALLOS
LYNN EINKAUF
STACEY FINCHER
MARY FLORES
MARIA GLYMPH
TOM GLYMPH
JOYCE HANNA
LEONORE HARMEL
BELINDA HILLHOUSE
CORKY HILLHOUSE
GAYLE HOFFER
SCOTT HOFFER
KEITH JONES
SANDY LAFORGE
CAROL LIPWORTH
STEVE LIPWORTH
LAURIE MCNAY
KERRI MORRISON
KAREN PENNER
MURRY PENNER
CYNTHIA PIRO
RON PUNNEO
BARRY PUTTERMAN
NANETTE PUTTERMAN
JON SHAFFER
AMY SKODA
STEPHEN SKODA
GAYLE WALDMAN
STEVE WALDMAN
BETH WALKER
JANE WEIL
STUART WEIL
ANNE WERNER
VICKI WEYEL

GREEN BEANS AND GUACAMOLE

GREEN BEANS & GUACAMOLE DONORS

THE ULTIMATE CHEF'S TABLE

APEX ENVIRONMENTAL, LLC

CORKY & BELINDA HILLHOUSE

PAUL HUDSON

SUPERIOR ENERGY

CULINARY CUISINE

JOYCE HANNA

STALLION OILFIELD SERVICES

THE ENTRÉE

SUSAN D. KROHN & PATRICK GEHM

TABLE D'HÔTE

MARGARET & CLARENCE CAZALOT

DAVID CLEMENT

SHELLY & CHRIS DEZEVALLOS

PAM & ED DEZEVALLOS

MARY & BILL FLORES

ROCHELLE & ALAN JACOBSON

LISA & TIM HARRIS

LISA & MARK LIVINGSTON

CARA & DON LOOPER

KAREN & MURRY PENNER

KAREN & CHUCK STALL

HORS D'OEUVRES

KRISTI & KEN BREAUX

KAYLYNN & PHIL CARPENTER

ROSE & HARRY CULLEN

LINDA & SIMON EYLES

LARRY FOSSI

BOB FUMAGALLI

MARGUERITE & BOB HAAS

TISSY & RUSTY HARDIN

ANUJA & NAVEEN JAGGI

GAYLE KINNIE

VICKI & STEVE KNOWLES

LIZ & SHANE MARCHAND

TIM MCGINTY

NANCY & LAMAR MCKAY

KATHY & TIM MITCHELL

ROXANNE & TIM NEUMANN

MARGARET OWEN

DEBBIE & JOE SLATTERY

BRIAN TEICHMAN

JOHN TURNER & JERRY FISCHER

MARGIE & THOM VENUS

VICKI & STEVE WEYEL

GAYE LYNN & STUART ZARROW

AMUSE BOUCHE

NANETTE & BRUCE ABRAMS

ILENE ALLEN

DONNA BODE

CANDACE BURNS

LISA CAMERON

GRACIE & BOB CAVNAR

DR. JOYA CHANDRA & TAYLOR CUTSHALL

JANET & WILL CRAVENS

LORETTA & LEE DERRICK

BETTY & PORTER DOBBINS

SHERRY & MIKE DUHON

LYNN EINKAUF

KATHLEEN & KEITH ELLISON

BETH & PHILLIP EVANS

LISA & MARK FERCHAU

STACEY FINCHER

MOLLY & CRAIG GLAUSER

PATTI & DAVID HANSON

ANNA HIGHNOTE

GRACE & DON ISON

MELISSA & SCOT ISON

CAROLYN LANDEN

LADEANNE & BOB LARSON

CAROL & STEVE LIPWORTH

KATE & JIM LYKES

MAURINE & JAY MANNING

LAURIE MCNAY

GARY MERCER

JUDY PENNER

HALLY POINDEXTER

SUSAN & ALAN RAFTE

JACK RAINS

REBECCA & DUDLEY RAY

AMY & STEPHEN SKODA

SIS & LONNIE SMITH

CINDY SOEFER

LINDA & ROARK ST. ROMAIN

CAROLINE & GREGG TYSON

GAYLE & STEVE WALDMAN

BETH & RAYMOND WALKER

MARK WENDELBURG

JANE & STUART WEIL

MELANIE & MIKE WEIR

RICHARD WHITE

SUZANNE & GARY WINKLER

SPONSORS WHO HELPED US ALONG THE WAY

AMY & STEPHEN SKODA

ARMANDO'S

BELINDA & CORKY HILLHOUSE

BELLA RINOVA

BENJY'S

BRICE REMALEY

CARRABBA'S

CRAPITTO'S

CAROL LIPWORTH DESIGNS

DEZEVALLOS FAMILIES

DONNA & TONY VALLONE

HARBORWALK YACHT CLUB

HOTEL GRANDUCA

HOUSTONIAN HOTEL, CLUB & SPA

INDIKA

JOYCE HANNA

JULIA EASLEY

JULIE SOEFER PHOTOGRAPHY

KAREN & CHUCK STALL

KATHY MITCHELL

KRISTI & KEN BREAUX

LADEANNE & BOB LARSON

LAURIE MCNAY

LE MISTRAL

LYNN EINKAUF

M PENNER

MARIA HURTADO

MARY & BILL FLORES

MIKE MOORE

PALOMINO BY BLANCA

RDG + BAR ANNIE

RAVENEAUX COUNTRY CLUB

RAYMOND J. WALKER, LLP

RAY'S COUNTRY GOURMET

REAL MEALS 365

REBECCA & DUDLEY RAY

ROBERT J. FUMAGALLI, P.C.

RUSTY HARDIN & ASSOCIATES

SALON VENDOME

SAMIR'S LIMOUSINE SERVICE

SORREL URBAN BISTRO

SORRENTO RISTORANTE

SWANTNER & GORDON

TONY'S

WEST HOUSTON AIRPORT

WILLIAMS & SONOMA

WILLOWICK COUNTRY CLUB

HELPFUL INFORMATION

RONI ATNIPP

RITA MILLS

BART NAY

APPENDIX

COCKTAIL SAUCE

1 CUP KETCHUP
2 TABLESPOONS PREPARED HORSERADISH
2 TABLESPOONS LEMON JUICE
SPLASH OF WORCESTERSHIRE SAUCE
DASH OF CAYENNE PEPPER

Combine all ingredients in a bowl. Mix well. Refrigerate at least one hour before serving to blend flavors.

NOTE: Adjust quantities to desired taste.

CROUTONS

3 TO 4 THICK BREAD SLICES, CUBED
2 TO 3 TABLESPOONS OLIVE OIL
SALT AND PEPPER
ADDITIONAL SEASONING, AS DESIRED

Preheat oven to 325°F.

In a large bowl, toss bread cubes with olive oil and seasoning. Spread on a baking sheet and toast in the oven, stirring often, until golden.

CULLEN'S CHICKEN STOCK

5 POUNDS CHICKEN BONES, RINSED WELL
¼ HEAD CELERY, CHOPPED
¼ BUNCH LEEK, CHOPPED
1¼ CUPS ONIONS, CHOPPED
¾ CUP CARROTS, PEELED AND CHOPPED
1 ROSEMARY SPRIG
1 THYME SPRIG
2 TABLESPOONS GARLIC CLOVES, CHOPPED
WATER

Place bones in a kettle and cover with water. Bring to a boil and skim. Reduce heat and simmer 3 hours, skimming often. Add remaining ingredients and cook for 1 hour. Strain through a sieve.

CULLEN'S VEAL STOCK

6 POUNDS VEAL BONES, ROASTED UNTIL GOLDEN AT 400°F
1 YELLOW ONION, CUT IN HALF AND CHARRED
2 TABLESPOONS OLIVE OIL
1½ CUPS CARROTS, CHOPPED
¼ HEAD CELERY, CHOPPED
1 LEEK, WASHED AND REMOVED OF ALL GRIT, CHOPPED
¼ YELLOW ONION, CHOPPED
1½ OUNCES GARLIC CLOVES
½ TEASPOON TOMATO PASTE
1 BAY LEAF
1 THYME SPRIG
1 ROSEMARY SPRIG
1 PINCH BLACK PEPPERCORNS
300 MILLILITERS RED WINE

Heat the olive oil in a large, shallow pot over medium-high heat. Add the carrots, celery, leek, onion and garlic. Caramelize vegetables, stirring often. Add the tomato paste, stirring until it begins to brown and caramelize. Add the wine and reduce. Add the veal bones and cover with water. Add the bay leaf, thyme, rosemary and peppercorns. Bring to a boil, then reduce heat. Simmer until reduced by half, skimming constantly. Remove from heat.

KIRAN'S GARAM MASALA

1 OUNCE CUMIN, WHOLE
1 OUNCE CORIANDER, WHOLE
½ OUNCE BLACK CARDAMOM, WHOLE
½ OUNCE GREEN CARDAMOM, WHOLE
½ OUNCE CLOVES, WHOLE
½ OUNCE BLACK PEPPERCORNS, WHOLE
½ OUNCE CINNAMON, WHOLE
½ OUNCE MACE, WHOLE

Combine all ingredients in coffee grinder until finely ground. Makes 5 ounces more than is needed in recipe. Store in the freezer for up to 1 year.

LEMON JUS

½ TABLESPOON OLIVE OIL
1 CLOVE GARLIC, MINCED
1 SHALLOT, MINCED
1 CUP LOW SODIUM CHICKEN BROTH
1 TEASPOON THYME
2 TABLESPOONS BUTTER, CHILLED AND CUBED
1 TABLESPOON FRESH LEMON JUICE
SALT AND PEPPER

Heat olive in a pan over medium heat. Add garlic and shallot and cook until softened, about 2 minutes. Stir in broth and thyme. Simmer until reduced to ¾ cup—about 5 minutes. Remove from heat. Whisk in the butter. Stir in the lemon juice and season with salt and pepper.

MASHED POTATOES

1 POUND POTATOES, RUSSET OR OTHER, PEELED
1½ TABLESPOONS BUTTER
½ CUP MILK
SALT AND PEPPER

In a pot large enough to hold the potatoes, add enough water to cover. Bring to a simmer and cook until tender. Remove from heat and drain. Return potatoes to pot, add butter and milk. Mash to desired consistency. Add more milk, if needed. Season with salt and pepper.

PICO DE GALLO

1½ POUNDS PLUM TOMATOES, SEEDED AND CHOPPED
¾ CUP ONION, CHOPPED
½ CUP CILANTRO, CHOPPED
3 TABLESPOONS LIME JUICE
3 TABLESPOONS JALAPEÑO, MINCED
1 CLOVE GARLIC, MINCED
SALT AND PEPPER

Combine all ingredients in a bowl.

TOMATO SAUCE

2 TABLESPOONS OLIVE OIL
1 ONION, DICED
2 TO 3 GARLIC CLOVES, MINCED
1 SPRIG OREGANO OR THYME
2, 28-OUNCE CANS WHOLE, PEELED TOMATOES WITH JUICE
SALT

Heat olive oil in a large saucepan over medium-low heat. Add onion and garlic and sauté until translucent, about 5 minutes. Add the tomatoes, herb sprig and a pinch of salt. Reduce heat to low, cook for approximately 1 hour, stirring and mashing tomatoes to break them down. Remove herb sprig.

INDEX

APPETIZERS

MEAT & POULTRY

SALADS & SOUPS

SEAFOOD

PASTA

SIDE DISHES

DESSERT

CREATIVE CONTRIBUTORS

BOOK DESIGN

● **GOOD PROJECT** | goodproject.com

Good Project is a full-service branding and design firm founded by husband-and-wife team, Matthew and Kimberly Pacetti. Both trained as creative professionals in New York City with backgrounds in marketing strategy, as well as graphic, product and multimedia design. Their award-winning work involves all aspects of their client's brand positioning in the market. Good Project collaborates with a varied set of clients ranging from large-scale health care systems to professional service companies to developers and start-ups. For the past 12 years, Good Project has been helping clients find a voice and presence that resonates with consumers. The team believes in telling a design story, keeping the message genuine and allowing the unique attributes of each project to shine through. Good Project's work is characterized by ambitious, creative thinking and purposeful design solutions.

WRITERS

● **MARIA GLYMPH** | mariaglymph.com

Maria Glymph is a writer and avid cook. She has authored creative works such as plays, poetry and stories, as well as written strategic plans, marketing materials and other business-related publications. Maria is currently working on a book of recipes based on her Greek heritage, as well as a monograph series based on her organizational development and strategic communications consulting practice. Maria is an advocate on behalf of the arts and is actively involved in the community.

● **NATALIE BOGAN MORGAN** | nataliebogan.com

Natalie Bogan Morgan is a Texas-based writer and editor. She is a graduate of the University of Kansas' William Allen White School of Journalism and specializes in lifestyle and marketing writing. She serves as editor of the Greater Houston Convention and Visitors Bureau's *Official Visitors Guide*, *Meeting Planners Guide* and *VisitHouston.com*. Her work has appeared in a variety of publications including *KC Weddings*, *Houston Brides* and Southwest Airlines' *Spirit* magazine.

PHOTOGRAPHY

SHANNON O'HARA | shannonohara.com

A childhood photography hobby helped jumpstart an international career for Houston-based lensman Shannon O'Hara. After growing up in Mississippi, Shannon earned a job as a Houston Ballet dancer, before studying at New York's International Center of Photography and The School of Visual Arts. After assisting top NYC photographers—including Bruce Davidson and Ben Fink—he returned to Houston, where he regularly shoots for *Houston* magazine and recently completed his first cookbook, *Energy Cuisine*. Shannon's work has appeared in a number of publications including *Budget Travel, Esquire, Gourmet and Garden and Gun.*

DEBORA SMAIL | realityphotography.net

Debora Smail is a New Mexico-raised, Texas-based freelance photographer and founder of Reality Photography. After attending Eastern New Mexico University, Debora settled in Texas, where she shoots regularly for Houston magazine and Texas Monthly. Her work has appeared on the cover of the coffee-table tome, *Knit Knit*, in several glossies including *National Geographic, Food & Wine* and *Vogue*, as well as national marketing campaigns for Schlumberger, CenterPoint Energy, Four Seasons Hotels and Café Express. Debora has also captured videos for local businesses and artists such as The Pioneers of Primetime TV and DJ Sun.

JULIE SOEFER | juliesoefer.com

Julie Soefer is a graduate of New York University's Tisch School of the Arts. She was the still photographer for the feature film *Supersize Me*, snapping the iconic movie-poster image of director Morgan Spurlock's mouth full of French fries. After years assisting one of her personal photography heroes, environmental portraitist Arnold Newman, Julie moved back to her hometown of Houston. Her work has been featured on the cover of *Houston* and *Modern Luxury Dallas* magazines, and she has contributed to *The Financial Times, Texas Monthly* and *The Wall Street Journal*. The Houston-based talent was named a 2011 finalist in Hearst Corporation's 8x10 Photography Biennial and recently released her first cookbook, *Lone Star Chefs*.